EARLY CHILDHOOD EDUCATION SERIES

Leslie R. Williams, Editor

ADVISORY BOARD: Barbara T. Bowman, Harriet K. Cuffaro, Stephanie Feeney, Doris Pronin Fromberg, Celia Genishi, Stacie G. Goffin, Dominic F. Gullo, Alice Sterling Honig, Elizabeth Jones, Gwen Morgan

(continued)

The View from the Little Chair in the Corner

Improving Teacher Practice and Early Childhood Learning

(Wisdom from an Experienced Classroom Observer)

CINDY RZASA BESS

Teachers College
Columbia University
New York and London

Published by Teachers College Press, 1234 Amsterdam Avenue, New York, NY 10027

Library of Congress Cataloging-in-Publication Data

Bess, Cindy Rzasa.
   The little chair in the corner : improving teacher practice and early childhood learning : (wisdom from an experienced classroom observer) / Cindy Rzasa Bess.
      p. cm. — (Early childhood education series)
   Includes bibliographical references and index.
   ISBN 978-0-8077-5039-1 (pbk. : alk. paper)
   ISBN 978-0-8077-5040-7 (hardcover : alk. paper)
      1. Learning. 2. Cognition in children. 3. Child development. I. Title.
   LB1060.B49   2010
   372.21—dc22   2009031658

ISBN 978-0-8077-5039-1 (paperback)
ISBN 978-0-8077-5040-7 (hardcover)

Printed on acid-free paper
Manufactured in the United States of America

17   16   15   14   13   12   11   10   8   7   6   5   4   3   2   1

Contents

Acknowledgments

My deepest thanks go to the teachers I learned from, worked beside, and watched perform over the years. Thank you for your great example and wonderful effort.

I am sincerely grateful to Marie Ellen Larcada, Senior Acquisitions Editor at Teachers College Press, for all the time and dedicated assistance she provided my project, but most importantly for the kindness, enthusiasm, and encouragement she personally extended to me. Thank you Wendy Schwartz, Development Editor, for all of the hard work and time you invested in this project. You truly made it better with each and every comment. I would like to thank Karl Nyberg, Senior Production Editor, for his thorough job finalizing this manuscript. I appreciate your kind support and guidance as I entered the final turn and headed for the homestretch.

Thank you John, Kara-Lynne, and Mackenzie Bess for all the reading and reviewing you did!

I dedicate this book to my husband,
John W. Bess,
my best friend and staunchest supporter.

Introduction

Teaching is both an art and a science; a multifaceted job that utilizes talent and skill, intuition and knowledge. Preschool teachers use their hearts and their heads throughout their day while working with young children. Accomplished preschool teachers merge their strong theoretical background, bolstered by factual knowledge, with their loving, nurturing hearts to effectively support young children. Having knowledge makes our practice strong, but having intuition makes our practice succeed.

In this book, we mesh theory with best practice, addressing not just the "whats" of theory and the "hows" of practice, but the "whys" behind both. When we fully comprehend why we are following certain practices and procedures, and understand the rationale for making good choices, we are being more than preschool teachers—we are being role models and setting good, strong examples. That is the role of a true teacher—not just acting the part, but fully being the part.

Part I, "The Early Childhood Education Context: The Children We Teach, the People We Are, and the Job We Do," provides a context for the preschool experience, and for early learning environments in general. Before we can understand the job of teaching, we must understand the young children in our care.

Chapter 1, "What Exactly Is Early Childhood?," looks at early child development from birth to approximately 5 years of age, and describes the typical child in easy-to-digest terms. By firmly grasping development, we can understand and appreciate the children in our care. Next is a brief look at the early learning environments available, examining young children as they adapt to them, and generally discussing the preschool teacher as he or she supports each child's adjustment from home to preschool.

Chapter 2, "Teachers Set the Stage for Learning," encourages teachers to gain a deeper appreciation for the job to enable more meaningful teaching. Offering a child an activity yields one outcome; knowing why we are offering it, and what the child will likely gain, yields a greater one. Linking understanding with effective planning produces meaningful learning.

The sum of our activities should not just produce a skill; it should end in knowledge. When we realize that we are doing more than offering tasks and making plans, we create a space from which an active learner, a capable child, a competent person, will emerge.

Chapter 3, "Supporting Teaching Practice Through Observation," dissects the experience into manageable pieces and fully examines the role of observation in the classroom. Great insight can be gained from looking at, listening to, and appreciating what transpires in the environment. By examining the information we gain from observation, we can identify areas that require attention, define a plan to make necessary changes, and improve the environment and experience for everyone.

Chapter 4, "Facilitating the Children's Preschool Experience Through Awareness," examines the importance of awareness in the teaching process. We need to understand what we personally bring to the classroom and how our attitudes and emotional tone impact it. We must be aware of our expectations regarding the children, know what is likely to happen developmentally, and define strategies so we are prepared for these moments. Lastly, we must be aware of the environment and make all necessary changes to ensure a safe setting.

Part II, "The Early Childhood Education Classroom Process: Daily Routines, Practices, and Materials," examines specific information that we can gain through observation of our daily activities, our routines and practices, our interpersonal interactions, and our classroom materials; helps teachers identify areas in need of attention and improvement; and defines strategies to enhance practice and raise the overall level of quality in a classroom.

We start at the root of good care—health and safety. Chapter 5, "Ensuring a Safe, Healthy, and Happy Classroom," and Chapter 6, "Best Teacher Practice—Establishing Sound Daily Routines," scrutinize these important aspects, which require a great deal of attention but are frequently overlooked. We must focus on these important points and meet higher standards; once we do, a battle for higher quality has been won.

Yet high quality demands more than health and safety. The environment and its materials must be stimulating and fun; hence, Chapters 7, "Enhancing Teaching Practice Through Effective Classroom Routines," and 8, "Creating the Optimal Center-Based Preschool Classroom."

Programs may supply materials and define curricula, but teachers provide opportunities. Chapter 9, "Maximizing the Center-Based Preschool Experience with Solid Teaching Practice," expounds upon strong teaching practice in a center-based program, and explains how combining interesting materials, insightful planning, and open-ended opportunities yields multilevel understanding in children.

Part III, "The Early Childhood Education Experience: Interpersonal Interactions," is where we apply reflection to our practice. Here the "whys" behind what we do are considered.

Chapter 10, "Creating Supportive Interpersonal Relationships in the Preschool," delves first into the importance of a teacher-child connection and discusses the interpersonal context from which functional and successful young children emerge. Then it examines the provisions made for the adults in a program and the "supports" provided to teachers and parents. When the classroom is clicking, that is one level of success; when the rapport between adults is productive, that is yet another level. The more positive the environment, the better it is for all.

We all make great choices! Some actions just deserve accolades—big fireworks and brass bands! Chapter 11, "Honorable Mentions and Memorable Moments," describes some of the best practices and most touching connections I have witnessed. If we adopted practices similar to these, the outcome would be great for *all*!

Part I

THE EARLY CHILDHOOD EDUCATION CONTEXT:

The Children We Teach, the People We Are, and the Job We Do

What Exactly Is Early Childhood?

The best way to prepare for a career in early childhood education is to understand child development and have a firm grasp of what children can do at different ages. Despite the fact that each child is an individual who follows his or her own maturational time frame, there is a typical path of development that all children follow (i.e., physical and developmental milestones, as well as points where capabilities and skills emerge as a child ages). Knowing what is typical in development and what is likely to happen over a given year of age enables a teacher to make insightful and effective plans for the children in the classroom. By being prepared to meet the different needs (e.g., physical, emotional, social, cognitive, and so forth) that accompany the varied ages, the teacher can create a caring environment that best suits the children in the group.

Early childhood is the period of time between birth and primary school, and it encompasses infancy, toddlerhood, the preschool years, and the beginning of elementary school (through 2nd grade). Most people specifically equate "early childhood" with the preschool years. For the purposes of this book, I will agree.

We learn our greatest life lessons during early childhood. Although they seem simple and obvious, to a small child every lesson is new, huge, and filled with obstacles. Consider that over this period a child will:

- learn to move through space (hopefully without crashing into things, which may cause injury or perpetual fear);
- adjust to an ever-expanding social world (from the womb to the immediate family to the extended family to early childhood care to school, and beyond);
- acquire and eventually manage an abstract communication system;

- encounter and come to understand complex interactions with new people (adults and children);
- discover and define an individualized self (complete with emotions that are strong and often confusing);
- successfully function in and adapt to the ever-changing dynamics of a greater and more demanding social role.

I often liken the early childhood period to a cupcake. We have to have a firm cupcake in hand before we can ice it—otherwise, we are just adding goo to goo. The early childhood period corresponds to the time when the cupcake is made (mixed, poured, and baked). It is the time when children learn about themselves, understand and follow rules, comply with adult directions, effectively express themselves, play well with others, and manage their behavior and emotions. A well-defined, competent, and functional child emerges, one who is ready to learn academic concepts and skills, such as learning letters, numbers, reading, and writing (i.e., the icing). Before children can learn "the extras," they have to know how to listen, how to function in a different environment, how to engage in new experiences, and how to interact with others. Yet ultimately they must come to know themselves.

Although all children are different, there is a common path that typical children follow as they grow and develop. There are milestones they reach, such as learning to walk, and general experiences they share, such as separation anxiety. As early childhood professionals, it is our job to understand development well enough to know what is happening at a given time and/or anticipate what is coming in the future, so we can effectively assist all children as they grow.

PUTTING TEMPERAMENT INTO PERSPECTIVE

One commonality shared by all children is temperament, an innate biological predisposition for dealing with the world. It is divided into three categories: easy, difficult, and slow to warm. "Easy" babies are a parent's dream, for they typically are not very demanding, they happily entertain themselves, and they are easy to care for (e.g., feed, change, stimulate, soothe, put to sleep, etc.). These babies smile a lot, are interactive, and are low-maintenance.

"Difficult" (or colicky) babies are a direct contrast, for they typically cry a lot, are harder to feed, often have trouble sleeping, cannot be soothed easily, and require a lot of time, attention, and trial-and-error approaches.

> **Point**—Upon entry to the preschool classroom, be sure to ask the parent to describe his or her child's temperament so contingency plans can be considered and developed before the child arrives the first day.

"Slow to warm" babies are easy to manage, but tend to have trouble with transitions. They often take a wait-and-see approach before making choices or entering into group settings and refrain from interacting with new adults or children until they feel comfortable. Yet, once acclimated, they easily fit into the group and the routine.

A BRIEF OVERVIEW OF EARLY CHILDHOOD DEVELOPMENT

All adults should understand development so they are prepared for the different ages and stages they will encounter with young children. Knowing what is typical allows adults to create an environment that supports the growth and experience of all children in the group and that is manageable, challenging, and productive.

Infants

Young infants are highly dependent, requiring care providers to feed, diaper, comfort, and stimulate them. Babies learn about the world through these interactions. To us, actions have specific purposes and meanings, yet infants experience them as a jumble of unrelated acts that just seem to happen to them. They have neither contextual experience nor temporal sense, preventing them from seeing connections between experiences—hence, their surprised expressions upon recognizing a familiar face. For them, the world is a magical place filled with unexpected events.

When handed objects, infants explore them through their only avenue of discovery—their senses. They mouth the object, touch it, look at it, and, with time, manipulate it (shake it, drop it, etc.). Each action yields a tiny bit of information about the world. Like the limited information they gain from their senses, their influence on the world is constrained by their restricted movement. Yet, once babies become mobile, everything changes. No longer are they dependent on others to move them around. They can sit upright on their own, creep, crawl, and then cruise. With each additional skill they develop, they have greater impact on their environment. They reach, grab, and touch things that previously were out of their range. They discover that their actions have power.

Think of how infants learn new skills. Before comprehending their ability to shape the environment, their inadvertent action may change it, such as striking a ball and making it roll away. They note the change and then intentionally repeat it a second time. They learn that their actions can alter their surroundings.

Picture an 11-month-old sitting in a high chair, the tray covered by many items (a teething ring, a rattle, a pacifier, etc.). He pushes them, they fall to the floor, and he looks over the edge. Then he picks up an item and drops it over the edge. He grins. He just discovered that *he* can make things happen. He intentionally drops another item and leans over to see it fall. His hand sweeps the tray and knocks everything to the floor. A huge smile follows. We respond with some form of acknowledgment: a smile, a word, a funny facial expression. He laughs. We retrieve the items and put them back on the tray. Swoosh—to the floor they go. The whole scenario repeats, yet this time, there is more to it. The child knows his power over objects and has discovered his power over *others*, too. By dropping these items to the floor, he can make us retrieve them. He learns the power of his action both physically and socially. He has a broader awareness of himself and his abilities now.

Similarly, during the latter part of their first year, infants make loose associations between objects and spoken words. They see the concrete object and hear the word *bottle* and soon learn to connect the two. As a result, when they want the object, they start to imitate the sound to let their parents know. Saying "ba-ba" demonstrates their understanding of the word-object connection. When adults respond by handing them the bottle, we acknowledge that connection and empower them to continue to acquire and express language. They come to discover the value of language to get results. They become more verbal and more interpersonally interactive.

Waddlers

Older infants who are just learning to walk (approximately 11 months to 15 months of age) become even more capable and volitional. They do things for the sheer delight of inducing change.

Initially, we help them manage their actions (e.g., take their first steps) and encourage them to try. While doing this, we aren't just building a skill; we are shaping a foundation for a fully developed person to emerge, one who is both socially connected and cognitively aware. He takes a step, we acknowledge it with a gleeful look, he feels accomplished, we cheer, and he realizes his newfound ability. A great deal is happening in this exchange for the child: The child has reached a physical milestone, experienced a sense of personal joy and power, achieved a point of competence, and shared a new kind of social connection. The skill was acquired in many developmental realms simultaneously.

When the child reaches her first birthday, we note a leap in language acquisition and self-expression. Since birth, she has heard words as fragments of sound, unintelligible and foreign. Over time and with repeated exposure, words become familiar and are associated with objects. With additional time, maturation, and effort, she utters a modified form, *bow-wow*, which we recognize and accordingly respond.

More occurs here than just the acquisition of words; the social component of language emerges. Prior to this, the child expressed herself through nonverbal cues, such as eye contact, facial expressions, and gestures. Now she can use verbal language to communicate, thus expanding her interpersonal interactions.

Through language, the young child's understanding of the world is further refined, and a hierarchical system for organizing knowledge begins to form. Verbal thought takes precedence over sensation-based organization, and words provide a context for arranging and comprehending experience. A profound system for learning slides into place and requires more and more information about the world. We must provide it.

The teaching role with children who are 1 year of age becomes very important now because we must provide for the child's social, emotional, and cognitive needs as well the physical ones (feeding, diapering, comforting). The child learns from our every word and action; we must make sure that all the information we provide them is good.

Toddlers

At this same time, more obvious expressive language starts to emerge and distinct attempts at words are discernible from the babble. Toddlers, from approximately 18 months to 2 years of age, use this new skill with great enthusiasm and emphatically use their two favorite words: "MINE!" and "NO!" Their newly acquired self-expression and their recently discovered empowerment underscore their emerging self. It won't be long before they are ready to join the preschool class.

2-Year-Olds

Most preschool programs do not consider 2-year-olds to be preschoolers; rather, they are often included in toddler programs. However, it is not uncommon for children who are "2.9" years old (i.e., September–December babies) to be included in "Threes" classes since they will be 3 years of age for the majority of the school year. Therefore, it may be prudent to review the typical development of 2-year-olds when preparing for a 3-year-old class so all bases are covered.

The average 2-year-old builds and adds new skills to his/her toddler foundation and thus becomes a multifaceted learner. Despite smaller stature and general awkwardness, the 2-year-old possesses a wide range of knowledge and skill: a rudimentary sense of self, an understanding that he or she is separate and distinct from others, a command of simple language (especially the words "No!" and "Mine!"), an ability to meet others' expectations (join the group for circle), a capability to complete self-help skills (get their coat), and an ability adapt to different environments (e.g., early childhood programs).

From 24 months on, 2-year-olds discover and define a sense of self with each new experience they attempt, accomplish, and master. They learn who they are, understand what they can do, and subsequently determine that they have a place in the "big" world.

The acquisition of language enables greater self-expression. They ask questions, talk more, and readily share their ideas with others. A broader foundation of language, gleaned from their daily life experience, enables thought to be hierarchically organized. For example, they might learn about dinosaurs and then subsequently classify each dinosaur as either big or small, meat-eater or plant-eater. After learning about animals in general, the children might organize each by habitat (farm, zoo, or household pet) or sound (moo, roar, quack, meow). This newly assembled cognitive hierarchy allows for greater learning, since more abstract representations are formed, which allows for broader knowledge. With each new addition to children's vocabulary, they develop an ability to think abstractly through the use of representations. No longer are they confined to using an actual cup when pretending to pour a liquid; now they substitute an available block in place of the cup and continue to play the game without affecting the outcome. Play becomes a means for discovery and a method for learning about the larger social world, which, in turn, promotes greater language development and higher-order thought.

However, the actual expression of language can frustrate children, for they often find their mouths out of sync with their minds. They more or less know what they want to say, but cannot quite say it. As a result, many 2-year-olds get frustrated when we do not understand them, and consequently resort to tantrums and/or biting. To forestall these moments, caregivers and teachers need to offer words and model them so children can see and hear how to express themselves verbally. For example, we can say, "I see you are frustrated that he took the fire engine from you. Ask him to give it back," or "You are sad because she hit you. Tell her not to hit you. Tell her you don't like that." When they scream at us to get our attention, we can acknowledge their wishes with, "You want me to sit with you? Okay, go pick out a book so we can sit together and read." Although these moments disrupt the group, a positive and compassionate response from the caregiver can quell some of the frustration, and modeling speech or offering words can also be helpful. Intervening here can make a difficult moment productive for all, and helping the child find the correct words can help him or her cope with frustration.

Caregivers of 2-year-olds assist these youngsters in acquiring and developing new social skills, thereby enabling them to understand themselves in the larger social context and discover their strengths and weaknesses in comparison to peers. Over time and with the support of adults in the child-care environment, 2-year-olds learn how to interact with others and come to better understand interpersonal relationships. Caregivers need to help them choose and use their words over physical acts of self-expression and assist them with sharing, taking turns, and being a part of a group experience. With time and experience, 2-year-olds mature into more adept social beings who are both ready and able to assimilate into a more formal preschool classroom setting.

3-Year-Olds

As they mature, 3-year-olds readily acquire personal self-help skills (e.g., toilet training) and adapt to different environments (e.g., early childhood programs). The growth and refinement of their vocabulary is significant, and as a result, they communicate their ideas easily. Rudimentary friendships form and develop. Their skill levels increase and they master new tasks. They become excited about learning, especially through exploration and discovery. They initiate new activities and try to become more self-sufficient at home and in school (e.g., they ask to pour their own juice or get dressed by themselves). However, their personal expectations and actual capabilities are often at odds, thus making them prone to moments of exasperation.

What can we expect from 3-year-olds? They want to "be" older so they try to act older, leading to a great deal of personal initiative. In order to better understand what is happening around them and to better understand the larger social world, they often ask the question "Why?" and engage in more conversation to share their knowledge. Three-year-olds also employ a lot of role-play, both with adults and with peers, to familiarize themselves with different perspectives. Lastly, they set out to master more skills and concepts, and achieve competence, often by watching a movie until they know it by heart and/or reading a story over and over again until they can recite it from memory.

What can they do physically? Three-year-olds are more adept and feel more accomplished at running, hopping, and skipping, often hollering "Look at me!" as they speed past. Or, they easily zoom around on the tricycle using pedals they could not previously reach. They can kick a ball and throw it *close* to where we are. We can clearly note how much they grew and changed over this year, especially when they climb the stairs using alternate feet, rather than going up one foot at a time as they did just the year before.

In addition, they have better fine-motor skills. Their eye-hand coordination has developed, so finer muscle movements are now possible with their hands and fingers. For instance, they can manipulate smaller puzzle pieces using their enhanced dexterity. They now write or draw using their fingers to hold the implement rather than their fist, and their wrists serve as the pivot point rather than their shoulder or elbow. They are more accomplished at pinching their fingers together and can use scissors (with help).

What is happening cognitively at this age? Quite a lot! Three-year-olds are highly verbal and express their ideas readily. They actively think about things now and ask a lot of questions to test their assumptions and fill in the gaps. Their vocabulary increases five-fold, generating an explosion in self-expression. They slowly learn the rules of grammar and try to correct their mistakes (*feet* versus *feets* or *foots*). Frequently, they engage in play scenarios that are creative, imaginative, and fantasy-oriented. Play is no longer done in a solo or parallel format, but now involves two or more children and is more complex, abstract, and internalized—that is, centered in representational thought, symbols, and action.

In addition, because of enhanced language capability, negative emotional outbursts (tantrums, defiance, and physical aggression) occur less frequently. Instead, 3-year-olds choose to use words and talk about their feelings and thoughts. Adults can assist them through this process by helping them choose words that effectively express their feelings, by modeling their use so a child hears how to speak, and by standing close to support them as they try new tactics. Many 3-year-olds become very effective negotiators once they learn to use words to their advantage. This is evident when they play games with their peers and set the rules for action.

Three-year-olds can "read" emotional tone and sarcasm, and can take another's perspective (in a limited way), allowing them to understand others' feelings. This newly discovered empathy prompts them to role-play and repeat situations that they have seen in effort to better understand events. Adults should encourage this activity; however, when necessary, they should be sure to correct any misconceptions the children hold. Doing so ensures that children obtain only good information about themselves, others, and the larger world overall.

Furthermore, a rudimentary understanding of time begins at this age. Children can follow the daily routine, anticipating what will happen next as well as predicting events based on experience and understanding the sequential order. For example, during the potty-training process, children learn to physically move to the bathroom, remove obstructing clothing (pants, underwear, shorts), use the toilet, and finally pull up their clothing. They know the sequence and thus are able to accomplish the task. This integrated knowledge helps them feel empowered and prompts them to try to do even more.

The anthem of the 3-year-old is "I can do it myself!" They like to learn new skills and will eagerly demonstrate them. They become independent, performing personal skills on their own, as well as making their own decisions. These attempts at mastery and self-determination have to be respected and encouraged.

Lastly, at the age of 3, children start to identify with their gender in an outward fashion. They openly can declare their status of "boy" or "girl" and use these labels to define themselves. They compare themselves with peers and talk about who they are in gender terms, as well as age and size (e.g., "I'm a big boy"). Knowing that they are male or female provides a starting point for defining likes and interests, which subsequently builds the foundation for greater social development and personality formation.

In the realm of social/emotional development, tremendous changes are taking place during this year. Three-year-olds engage with others and ask for assistance when needed. Empathy and altruism are evident, now that they can assume the limited perspectives of others. They become more cooperative with peers, because they understand that they need to behave in a prosocial way to get and keep their friendships, which solidify over time, and tend to follow same-sex patterns.

Needless to say, they occasionally have tantrums to make their point, especially when they have difficulty fully expressing themselves. Problems with self-expression can be due in part to minor developmental delay, temperament and personality style, imitation of observed peer behaviors, and a result of learned behavior that has been rewarded in the past whether at home or elsewhere.

As their exposure to the larger social world increases, their need to be "first" or "right" diminishes, and they learn instead to take turns and share. They are more socially adept, interact well with others, enjoy new social play scenarios, and cooperatively engage with peers and adults. They invest more in being a part of a group and readily make an impact in their social world. Adults can effectively teach young children how to see the larger perspective through role-modeling and occasional intervention. Three-year-olds are emotionally resilient and, even at such a tender age, they are able to bounce back from small hardships and tough moments, provided that they are given care and support.

4-Year-Olds

Sometimes people underestimate a child's capabilities. To many adults, children appear young and inexperienced due to the vulnerability and tentativeness they exhibit when learning new skills or adjusting to new situations. Don't be fooled!

Four-year-olds are very self-aware, honing their social skills and possessing a greater understanding of the larger social world. They develop friendships based on perceived personal similarities and find commonalties between themselves and others. They actively observe and readily learn from their social environment. They ably adapt their social skills to new situations and are accomplished communicators, both verbally and physically.

Skills that 4-year-olds enjoy include an extensive vocabulary; an acute ability to read body language, facial expression, tone of voice, and gestures; and the ability to both use and understand nuances in speech. Their level of cognitive complexity allows them to think more abstractly. They now use language, a powerful tool, to establish their place in the social hierarchy, as is evident in the common classroom utterances "You're not my friend!" or "You're not coming to my birthday party!" Language allows them to impose their will on others and/or assists them in getting their way through statements such as "You better help me clean up or I'll tell." Yet, although they ably dish out disrespect, they often have difficulty receiving similar statements and may burst into tears when they are called "crybaby."

They skillfully utilize language to make their point, but they have yet to understand the ramifications and social consequences of their words. Adults can guide children in their social interactions and assist them in choosing the proper words to convey their points. When a child makes a poor choice of words, uses mean-spirited speech, or adopts a harsh tone, the teacher must deal with these moments quickly to keep emotional outbursts and deeply hurt feelings to a minimum. With time, social guidance, and experience, children learn to temper their language so that a more harmonious experience results—until the next power struggle occurs.

Four-year-olds learn best through direct experience and hands-on learning opportunities, yielding skill levels that approach mastery in social and cognitive areas. They initiate new games in small and large groups. They define their own rules and can function within them in a cooperative way. Furthermore, 4-year-olds have become personally more self-aware, somewhat introspective, and better able to understand themselves and others—peers and adults alike. They form friendships more easily at this time because they are learning to see beyond their own limited perspective and can adopt other people's points of view. They become "rational social interacters."

Four-year-olds are emotionally resilient, taking both challenges and triumphs in stride. In addition, they can adjust to difficult situations that take place in their family (e.g., parental divorce, the death of a family member), develop effective coping methods, and, with social support, continue to go on to have fruitful lives. They are developing emotional strengths and capabilities that will aid them as they move from the relative protection of the home and preschool environments to the broader social world.

5-Year-Olds

The age of 5 is a pivotal point in child development. The child has accumulated a great deal of self-knowledge and is now able to effectively define him- or herself. Children of 5 have a better handle on their recent physical transformation, cognitive changes, and social and emotional development. Thus, they have a comfortable understanding of the self.

Physically, 5-year-olds are more accomplished and can demonstrate competence in many gross-motor skills (e.g., easily hop and skip), although emerging abilities still need work (e.g., throwing or catching a ball). They can play organized sports with much adult supervision, and they more or less follow instructions and work as a team. Many 5-year-olds show improved fine-motor coordination, have become proficient in the use of scissors and writing instruments, and can focus on what they are writing rather than managing the movement of the implement.

Cognitively, 5-year-olds think in an operational manner and can see relationships that were unexplainable in the past. For example, they understand rudimentary conservation principles (e.g., number); have greater command of language, using correct inflections, tense, plurals, and so forth; can follow more complicated directives; and are able to create and develop complex games and play scenarios with their friends, which indicates a wider imagination. Furthermore, they can identify their gender with certainty, and they assume roles and actions that are in line with their understanding of gender. Lastly, they define themselves by comparing their own skills, proficiencies, and physical attributes with those of others.

Five-year-olds are more socially and emotionally aware of themselves and know what they like, dislike, want to do, and can do. They form their own ideas and express them easily. They communicate clearly and directly, frequently ask questions, and engage their peers and adults (even unfamiliar ones) in conversation. In addition, they exhibit higher sensitivity to the social world, and in return, are influenced by it and by others who are in it. They have a better appreciation for words and actions, and they can discern discrepancies and/or inconsistencies in the actions of others.

In light of their emerging competence, 5-year-olds feel capable, and they willingly enter new arenas, such as joining a sports team or mastering a new skill, such as learning to dance, doing martial arts, or ice skating. They are confident in what they can do, know how they feel, and are able to express themselves to get desired results. With age and greater personal experience, they are becoming self-reliant.

Experience has provided a better understanding of who they are and what they are capable of doing due to the new situations and experiences. They have mastered many skills and have acquired a large and functional vocabulary that they use proficiently. They are aware of their strengths and weaknesses as a direct result of the many comparisons that *they* have made between themselves and others. At this point, they not only have more information available about themselves, but they can make sense of it and use it to their advantage.

Nonetheless, 5-year-olds must still rely on others for guidance and direction. Fears and concerns appear due to an understanding of more abstract concepts. For example, some children are afraid to make mistakes and refrain from performing new skills or making decisions. Some children fear the unknown and consequently become afraid of the dark, dislike being alone, and worry about "monsters" in the closet or under the bed. They become aware of what they "don't know," which can, at times, overwhelm them. Although they are competent in many areas, they still experience moments when they feel out of control and anxious. They are growing up, but they are not yet grown-up.

Thus, 5-year-olds are the yin and yang of child development—both independent and dependent, self-expressive and tongue-tied, confidently self-aware and self-consciously aware of others, self-centered as well as thoughtful and altruistic, attentively focused and uncontrollably energetic. An adult's duty is to help them find balance when they swing out of control and assist them in making successful adjustments to restore a sense of control and calm.

As adults and as teachers, we should envision ourselves as the fulcrum of a seesaw. *We* provide the point for balance to occur. Without the fulcrum, the seesaw lies flat on the ground. Without a variety of experiences, a child cannot know him- or herself. Like a seesaw, a young child swings widely from one extreme to the other with little control, bumping hard on the ground at times or swooshing wildly through the air at others. We need to remember that we are their fulcrum when they independently push us away, then cry when we are not there. We must remember that we are their fulcrum when they seem so self-assured during the day and so afraid at night, or so afraid at school and so confident at home. We need to remember that we are their fulcrum when they act cocky in front of us and clumsy in front of their peers. We must remember that we are their fulcrum when they are sweet and cuddly with us one minute and surly when they are with their friends. We restore the balance for children when they swing into unknown places beyond their realm of comfort. They depend on us to be there for them, when they want us and even when they do not.

Five-year-olds are self-aware, aware of others, self-conscious, defiant, independent, comparative, adeptly verbal, compliant, and assertive. They are becoming socially competent human beings.

Now that we have a handle on the children, let's look at the way the preschool experience addresses their needs and supports their learning.

DOVETAILING THE YOUNG CHILD WITH PRESCHOOL

The goal for children during this formative period is to realize the basics of being a person by learning through their interactions with the world and forming a social self. This is a period for socialization. Yet, when preschool programs primarily focus on learning numbers, letters, reading, and writing in an effort to build academic skill, they miss the *true goal* of early childhood. Preschool teachers must emphasize the value of "being" during early childhood more than focusing on the "doing" of childhood. After all, they are developing human *beings*, not human *doings*.

A variety of early childhood education (ECE) settings exists (e.g., nursery schools, preschools, early learning centers, Head Start and School Readiness programs), and they provide more than simple child care. They have structured educational programs in place that follow a specific curriculum and provide young children with opportunities to learn, explore, and play under the tutelage of teachers who are knowledgeable in the early childhood realm.

EARLY CHILDHOOD EDUCATION SETTINGS

Early childhood education programs (e.g., preschools, nursery schools, and extended-day early learning programs) help construct a competent child by offering opportunities that promote self-awareness and self-discovery as well as interpersonal experiences and knowledge of the wider world.

Traditionally, nursery schools provided a context for very young children, 2 to 4 years of age, to gain social experiences for short periods (e.g., 2½- to 3-hour morning and afternoon sessions), before entering formal kindergarten programs. Today, preschool programs may operate for longer time frames (e.g., 5½ to 6 hours of classroom time), conforming to the standard school day. In addition, Early Learning Centers often exist within child-care settings, operating for 8 or more hours, to support full-time working families and provide educational experiences that prepare young children for entry to public school. School Readiness and Head Start programs often adopt this longer-day time frame and adhere to specific standards defined for the early childhood education experience by either the state or federal government.

The best time to introduce concepts and skills to young children is when they are ready for, and capable of, learning them. Force-fed, rote learning is failure-driven, whereas developmentally appropriate and personally meaningful learning is success-driven. Child-initiated, hands-on experience tends to induce the best learning. Conversely, hearing about a subject, concept, or skill often has less impact.

Teachers should consider the *actual* age of each child when working with preschoolers. As teachers, we often refer to our classes by their age range (e.g., the "threes" class or the "fours" class). This makes sense because, collectively, the children span a specific year of developmental age. However, we must constantly remind ourselves that, within this group, the actual ages of the children can vary greatly. For example, within a typical "threes" class (i.e., 36 months or thereabout), there may be children who have not yet turned 3 (e.g., 2.9 years) as well as those who are nearly 4 years of age. Therefore, the age range might technically span from 33 months to 47 months of age during the term.

Some preschools try to cluster children and have groups designated as "young threes" or "older threes" to reduce the age spread within the group. By accounting for the children's ages in months rather than in years, teachers can have more accurate expectations and, thus, can define developmentally appropriate plans for individual children as well as for the class overall. It also reminds us to be more supportive as children adapt to new environments and adjust socially, since changes may prove more difficult for the younger ones.

Despite their age group, remember that the children we teach and care for are young, vulnerable, and in need of some security, such as a hand to hold or a gentle hug. These young children require clear direction in the form of specified classroom rules, as well as simple behavioral reminders and guidance to keep them safe. If their lifetime experience can be quantified in terms of months of learning, they have no real context from which to draw when making choices, especially in a new environment. All young children require attentive supervision and direction to acclimate successfully to the bigger social world.

In many ways, teachers are like mother ducks leading a train of ducklings. We are responsible for protecting and leading our charges safely through the day because we know what to expect. We have been through this territory before and have developed a contextual understanding of it. We have accumulated experience that has taught us what is hazardous and what is safe. We know when to cross the road and when to wait. We show them the way, and our ducklings follow our lead. It is an awesome responsibility, one that should not be taken lightly.

Now consider the same scenario from the perspective of the ducklings. They are completely new to their surroundings. The only place they have known previously is their nest. The world is big and sometimes frightening. They have no context yet to help them make sense of what they are doing or where they are, so they follow Mother Duck's lead.

As teachers, we become "security blankets" for the children in our care. We help them adjust to new social relationships by providing guidance, offering information to help them make sense of their experiences, and comforting them when they become fearful, tired, or frustrated. We teach through example, help them make good choices, understand their emotional reactions, and forge new relationships.

As they enter the preschool environment, many young children are making their initial transition from the safety of the home and the care of familiar adults to a larger social world comprised of new adults, new friends, new surroundings, new toys, and a void that Mommy or Daddy once filled. Some have little or no experience with other children outside of an occasional playdate or a sibling relationship, making the abrupt change overwhelming for many children.

We need to offer comfort when the daily experience proves to be too much for them, create a safe environment so no one gets hurt, help the children separate from the familiar and transition to the new, and keep them stimulated and engaged in novel learning opportunities. Such support ensures that each child will eagerly want to discover and experience the larger world.

In conclusion, a great deal of change occurs over the first 5 years of development. When young children enter early learning settings, they need teachers who firmly grasp general early child development. They also require caregivers who can aid in their emotional development by supplying patient, nurturing, and compassionate care. In addition, young children must have teachers who support language acquisition and self-expression as well as provide contextual information, offer meaningful learning opportunities, and support skill acquisition and mastery, which enhance cognitive development. Lastly, infants, toddlers, and preschoolers need adults who can augment their social development by helping them integrate into peer groups, develop and manage friendships, and follow adult direction. We need to be there to assist them through their many and varied experiences and help them make the journey the best it can be.

Teachers Set the Stage for Learning

2

As teachers, we understand the importance of being active learners. We know our teaching is most effective when we stay current in the field and learn as much as we can. Only when we have a firm foundation of knowledge, a solid rationale that supports its implementation and expertise in imparting it, can we successfully teach children and help them grow, develop, and flourish.

Teachers who take their job seriously are ready to learn, willing to share their knowledge, and ably offer insights to their students. But why? The answers are as diverse as the teachers questioned, yet three central reasons emerge: They love learning, they believe that knowledge and success in later life go hand-in-hand, and they care about children and want to help them grow through education.

Teachers share a few common qualities: First, they often are other-oriented, and thus, they like all types of people and are able to work with most of them. Second, they frequently have generous spirits and freely give their time to help others learn and master new ideas, concepts, and skills. Third, they are effective synthesizers, taking familiar concepts and rethinking them using "out-of-the-box" methods, thus yielding new results and/or deeper understanding. Lastly, they are effective communicators, and can enthusiastically impart synthesized ideas in ways that are meaningful and interesting to others.

WHO CHOOSES TO WORK WITH YOUNG CHILDREN?

Teachers who work with young children have additional attributes that make them suited for this type of work, such as patience, nurturance, kindness, and generosity of spirit. Preschool teachers want to make a difference in the lives of young children by supporting their emerging self-knowledge, by providing them with opportunities to gain new skills and acquire new concepts, and by assisting them as they make sense of the bigger world. It is an awesome task that teachers have willingly undertaken, but the work has its perks! On a daily, sometimes hourly, basis, teachers receive enthusiastic greetings and warm hugs. Little eyes sparkle brightly at them and huge smiles greet them. Laughter reigns in the classroom and teachers are enveloped in innocence. Each new discovery shines in the children's faces and, as they master new skills, teachers share in the revelry of the statement, "I DID IT!"

In many ways, a teacher is like a refreshing well, one where people stop to quench their thirst. A good well has depth, clear and fresh water, and is easy to access. Over the course of a day, many children dip into teachers' "water" and drink from their spring. Children quench their thirst and rest at their teacher's side. The secret to attracting "drinkers" is to stay deep, fresh, and easy to access. There are many wells out there that have run dry. Many have stale and stagnant water. Many are difficult to reach or hidden from use. But not us. We want to know more, stay current, and make a difference.

INTEGRATING A TEACHER'S EDUCATION

In today's world, experience needs to be coupled with education. Many who currently work in the field came to it as parents or grandparents with a lot of personal knowledge in tow. Many have returned to school to learn the latest advances in early childhood education concepts, practices, and strategies. Others, fresh out of school, bring with them solid theory and practice. Regardless of our point on the line of experience, our personal knowledge must stay current. Just like the children, we must remain active learners. So much awaits our discovery.

How do we stay current, fresh, and on the edge of what we need to know to be successful teachers? We must learn, listen, watch, question, and try new things. We must synthesize what we already know with what we are learning, and, after cognitively *knowing* it, we must reprocess it through an emotional filter so we *feel* it as well. What we cognitively understand, we must also intuitively realize. Truly gifted teachers merge the two together and function from a place where head and heart work in tandem. When we are in that space, we have depth; thinking and feeling blend into understanding.

While working with young children, we must resist functioning in a single dimension. Although it may seem prudent to just think when completing tasks, defining plans, introducing a new topic, or demonstrating a skill, or it may seem appropriate to feel for or empathize with a sad or hurt child, most of the time we have to consciously be present in three realms simultaneously: the cognitive, the emotional, and the social.

Having a disconnect between the head and heart has created most of the world's problems. When we act impulsively without thought or act dispassionately without feeling, we avoid meeting life's challenges. When we act unidimensionally, we often stumble, fall, or even fail because we do not consider all the ramifications of our choices or actions. We get the wrong outcome. Yet, when we unite head and heart and bring them fully to bear, then we are present in the moment and can make a difference.

BUILDING KNOWLEDGE

When we comprehend a new concept, strategy, or idea, or when we learn a skill, we have gained one level of learning, a type of basic or surface knowledge. We see this daily when young children count to 10 by rote and/or recite the alphabet. They rattle off the information, but do not grasp the underlying significance. They may know how to repeat a sequence, but they miss the grander concepts that rest beneath it. In a way, it is like the wooden frame into which a concrete foundation is poured. True understanding, like the poured cement, comes when we learn new information, synthesize it so it becomes personally meaningful, and then integrate it with what we know. This has a cumulative effect because it fills in the gaps and creates a firm base on which additional knowledge will rest.

As we all have discovered, the acquisition of knowledge or a skill can sometimes result from mere happenstance. For example, we discover a new travel route by accident after making a wrong turn while driving. We happen onto a new route, and this surface information helps us briefly. However, it is only after we incorporate it into our working knowledge of the local streets in our community that it takes on enhanced value, offering us an alternate route where there was none previously.

Learning results from change. Change is constant for young children, and they mature and develop in many areas simultaneously. Across a brief period, we can witness physical transformation, emotional growth, social development, cognitive comprehension, skill acquisition, and personal understanding in our children. As these individual parts unite into a greater developmental "whole," learning can occur.

When we acknowledge that, regardless of age, we *all* grow and benefit from our accumulated experience, we better comprehend our role as teachers. We are not just investing in our children's brains, but in their whole selves. We need to teach at many levels concurrently in order for strong understanding to emerge and grow. We must give our preschoolers information on how to make choices, offer opportunities so they can define and know their capabilities, and provide hands-on experience for acquiring and honing new skills. In addition, we must encourage them, reflect their accomplishments in *our* faces when they succeed, be emotionally available to them, and support and nurture their emerging sense of self.

We need to be present in a way that utilizes both our thoughts and our feelings. We need to be in close proximity, seated in a chair or on the floor and not observing from a distance. We need to be actively invested in what is happening with a child, a small group, or the larger class overall, by observing children as they work and play, listening to their interactions, asking questions to understand what they are doing, and being available to them to model a skill. When we interact, we need to be aware of what we are doing and what impact we are having. We should be on the same level and make eye contact when we speak. We should be cognizant of our body language and know what messages we are sending through it, making sure that those messages are positive and productive rather than judgmental or intimidating. We need to be compassionate and connected to the children so we can be fully engaged and truly teach.

MAKING LEARNING OPPORTUNITIES CHILD-FRIENDLY

Children benefit most from classroom environments that are child-friendly and developmentally appropriate, ones that prepare them socially and challenge them cognitively. Child-centered play-based programs invite child-initiated action, offer meaningful learning experiences, and provide opportunities that interest children. Active interaction and exploration afford the best learning outcomes, because opening the door to personal initiative and discovery has a greater effect than just showing children a result. Through hands-on learning, children become excited and intrigued by new opportunities, focus on what they are doing in order to make sense of it, encounter new problems, apply themselves while solving them, and then relish the discoveries they have made along the way.

Preschool teachers should offer stimulating materials and present opportunities that encourage children to work, play, and learn together. Teachers should allow the children to set their own goal, define their own plan, and work in their combined way to solve a problem, acquire a skill, or learn a concept as a team. A teacher should facilitate children's learning but not formally teach a lesson; instead, the teacher should encourage the children to exchange ideas and "think outside the box," thereby bolstering their interpersonal communication and strengthening their thinking

> **Point**—Capitalize on the interests and experiences of children. Foster active learning by providing exciting and novel opportunities, then step back and let children discover the world on their own.

and reasoning skills. The greatest discoveries teachers relish are those that result from either tenacious perseverance and/or insightful trial-and-error learning. By-products of this approach are that children discover how to work together, understand the value of listening to and communicating with others, learn to take turns and share materials, and form a basis from which friendships can take root and grow.

Consider this example: A teacher defines "mixing secondary colors from primary colors" as the daily activity and places primary color watercolor paints, eye droppers, and coffee filters on the table. A child drips the diluted paint onto the porous paper and watches it diffuse. He does it again and again. He never mixes the colors as the teacher intended, yet a scientist is born. Was her project a failure? No! Meaningful and productive learning resulted, even though it was unplanned. The child's discovery and enthusiasm fueled a unit on the diffusing of liquid through celery stalks, long-stemmed white carnations, paper towels, and so on. Sometimes a new learner can be the best teacher. It just takes the right combination of materials and opportunities to make a center "pop."

Each child possesses his or her own abilities, interests, and level of skill. Therefore, each area's materials should reflect a range of possibilities that reflect the group. Teachers should encourage children to take different approaches and note their unique styles during an observation, utilizing the information when planning for individual children and for the overall group.

PROVIDING MATERIALS THAT INCLUDE, INTEREST, AND ENGAGE

Fun and manageable materials should be placed in each learning center. The activities and materials ought to lead to feelings of success and

> **Point**—The preschool classroom provides more than just learning opportunities for young children. It also has the potential to stir a child's imagination and spur creative expression. The secret to success is to open the possibilities to include just about any topic of interest.

accomplishment rather than failure. Therefore, teachers should provide items ranging in skill level, such as puzzles. If the class is made up of 3- and 4-year-olds, the puzzles should span a wide range of ability. A few puzzles with large and small knobbed pieces should be offered for younger children, who are still developing their coordinating eye-hand movements and fine-motor skills. It is also good to include some wooden picture puzzles as well as simple form puzzles where a single piece fits into its own place. For more accomplished puzzle makers, floor puzzles should be available. For mathematically talented children, teachers should supply geometric puzzles with varying size, shape, and color components. Teachers should consider the puzzle-builder and put out the best matches.

Materials should not be retired too quickly; keep a few old favorites around for those moments when children's self-esteem needs a boost. We all know that when a child has a particularly hard day, feels miserable about his abilities, and tries but does not succeed (e.g., his block tower falls over, his LEGO car won't roll, his letters go in the wrong direction), he can use a real ego boost. Be sensitive and proactive. Retrieve his favorite puzzle, one that he mastered long ago, and sit with him as he dumps it out and puts it together lickety-split. Share in this moment and encourage him to do it again. By effectively using this old friend, a teacher can help him get back on the track for success.

CREATING A CENTER-BASED ENVIRONMENT

A center-based curriculum provides a means to an end for all areas of human development (i.e., social, emotional, cognitive, language, and physical). Centers should be set up so that a variety of activities can occur in the classroom at the same time. Within the classroom there should be art, music, and dramatic play areas to enable creative self-expression and role-playing, as well as a building center with blocks or interconnecting materials to indirectly teach children pre-science and pre-math. A section should also be set aside where children can use manipulatives and/or puzzles to develop fine-motor skills. There should also be a place to retreat for quiet time and reflection. A designated writing center, book nook, and listening corner should be offered to promote language and support literacy, and a discovery center with science, nature, math, and number items should be accessible to encourage problem solving and abstract thinking. Lastly, sensory tables should be available to acquaint young children with different textures (e.g., gravel, mud, cornmeal) and media (e.g., sand, water, rice) and to help form conceptual knowledge. A more in-depth examination of each center follows in Chapter 8. Providing strong centers for exploration supports independent hands-on learning and facilitates the development of new, personally meaningful concepts, skills, and insights.

Teachers foster a natural flow when setting up the room and the materials. Would a child use small building toys to supplement a block-building project? Probably—so these centers should be placed near one another. Would a child need paper and pencils in the dramatic play area to prepare a shopping list while pretending to go to the store? Yes—so those materials should be placed there. Teachers can take it one step further and connect the writing center with the dramatic play area so children can "go to work" in the writing center and then "come home" to the dramatic play area. If the centers fit with one another, place them near each other.

Noise level should also be considered when arranging the room. Louder centers such as blocks and dramatic play should be kept together in one area, and a quieter center, such as the book nook, should be in another area. Teachers should seriously consider the placement of the classroom computers; if children blast the volume, they should be moved away from the listening center and library to limit frustration and angry outbursts.

When arranging the room, consider the number of children who are likely to use each center as well as its dynamics. For the more active areas, larger spaces should be set aside. A block area should accommodate three or four children and their structures. If we set aside a confined space, towers will likely tumble and peers will travel through one another's work zones. Smaller areas can be used to accommodate quieter pursuits (e.g., book nook, writing/listening centers), since fewer children will be there at any one time.

Classroom materials should change periodically. New ones should be added and worn ones switched out. Teachers should regularly transform the dramatic play area to elicit new role-playing (e.g., have a doctor's office one month, a restaurant another, a post office, a pet hospital, and a shoe store the next). Different children will gravitate to the area based on what is available and what they like. A lot can be gained through a little variety.

Lastly, teachers should *always* keep safety in mind when arranging the furnishings and setting up the classroom space. The children must be easily supervised from every vantage point in the room.

Once the environment is ready, we must introduce high-quality teaching to it. Every day, we enter our rooms and prepare for the learning of the day. We know our children and understand what they can do. We have defined our goals for each child and our objectives for the whole group. We have outlined lesson plans that will be interesting and stimulate the children to discover, play, and learn. We have developed solid child-friendly activities to support their learning. Once the stage is set and the curtains rise, we need to get ready for the role of a lifetime teacher. We must fully assume our part as teacher, caregiver, social support, language-builder, "security blanket," and role model. We set the stage for learning. Now let's fully engage in our part.

LEVELS OF TEACHERS—LEVELS OF TEACHING

Some teachers are very good at executing specific tasks, such as setting up snacks and putting out materials. That is the most basic level of good practice. Others are good at fitting tasks together to make good experiences. That is the next hierarchical level of good practice. Others integrate planning and execution so that tasks are meaningful to the children, which is the third level of good practice. But the teacher who can do all of that as well as understand the reasoning and rationale for doing it all in the first place is functioning at the greatest level of teaching practice. See Figure 2.1.

In my experience, being a warm body is the most rudimentary level of teaching. We all have encountered the people who are present in the classroom but are not doing much more than generating heat. We all know "teachers" who sit with the children in the book nook or at a table, but do

FIGURE 2.1. Levels of Teaching Practice

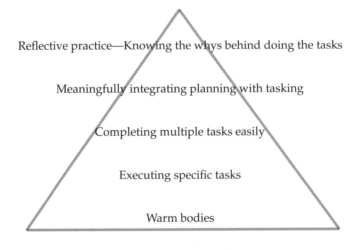

Reflective practice—Knowing the whys behind doing the tasks

Meaningfully integrating planning with tasking

Completing multiple tasks easily

Executing specific tasks

Warm bodies

not read or interact with them, or who stand around the play spaces, but do not really monitor the activity or supervise the children's behavior. We all know teachers who are physically present but are not emotionally or cognitively there. They help maintain the adult-child ratio and collect a paycheck. But are they invested in the children's learning or experience? Not really. As a result, in the pyramid of good practice, they are in the basement.

At the most *basic* level of practice, some teachers perform tasks and possess teaching skills, but do their job at a superficial level. They work passively; they do not take the bull by the horns. In some programs, these people tend to the chores, such as assisting children with toileting or serving as a placeholder with children—they read stories to individuals or small groups not to teach but only to keep the children occupied.

Some teachers attain the level of *good* practice when they ably execute many tasks simultaneously and yield a good outcome. They invest themselves in learning opportunities but focus more on the process and less on the interactions that take place around them. They do a good job and know what to do, but they still may be somewhat disengaged from the children or the overall meaning of their job. A teacher may read a story to a group of children and ask general questions that trigger rote responses, such as "The author is the person who?" Such teachers still need to make the jump to connecting the task with the ultimately desired outcome: enthusiastic learning by the children.

Some teachers plan out effective programs and incorporate different materials to supplement learning, indicating *great* practice. These teachers consider the various aspects of developmental learning (e.g., physical, social, emotional, and cognitive) when making plans, and consider the levels of skill and interest of the children so that the newly introduced activity will attract and involve most, if not all, of them. The teacher may read an interesting book to the group and then elicit personal stories that relate, directly or indirectly, to the text.

Teachers who exhibit *excellent* practice succeed in all these areas and "get it" at all levels. They aptly integrate their planning with suitable materials to produce personally meaningful learning experiences for each child and for the group overall. They know their children (e.g., their likes, dislikes, and interests) and thus maximize children's learning experiences. These teachers make individualized plans for each child so the children can excel or build competence across centers. Furthermore, these excellent teachers effectively manage the teaching team members to utilize the strengths of every classroom teacher, so each puts forth their best effort and makes the process work across the board. This kind of teacher would not just read a book with the group; he or she would discuss it, get the children's feedback, write and illustrate a class-made book using the children's responses and drawings, and then place it in the book nook or offer it to the children's families in the lending library.

Excellent teachers are fully present in each activity and are invested in the children they are engaging. They are always prepared for new learning opportunities and adeptly incorporate those opportunities into future lesson plans. Excellent teachers shine during the day and encourage co-workers and children to shine as well. They flexibly implement a plan and know when to scrap it when it is not working or put it temporarily aside if something better turns up. They also turn adversity into opportunity and hardship into a learning moment. Finally, they seize each day, so few teachable moments are missed.

Every teacher can be an excellent teacher—many already are. We just need to actively choose to be excellent each and every moment. Let's affirm to ourselves that we will be the best we can be—and the best for the children. In the classroom setting, we are not only teaching; we are also learning with, and through, the children. We should relish these moments, enjoy the challenges, and consciously realize how important we are as we do our job.

An excellent teacher is proactive in what he or she does and is aware of what he or she models. These teachers show children how to be thoughtful rather than impulsive in their actions and words. They lead by example.

We manage all of our daily experience in three ways: by *acting, interacting,* or *reacting.* When we *act,* we think while we perform a task. For example, we need to get a pencil, so we move our hand toward it, grip it with our fingers, and pick it up. We act with intention. When we *interact* with others, we think while communicating. We think about what we want to convey, monitor our speech, and gauge the other person's response. If something is unclear, we restate the point. We interact with careful thought and deliberation. Being thoughtful, intentional, and deliberate means we are in control of what we are saying and doing. Conversely, when we *react* to situations or people, we respond impulsively. Our reactions are rash and impetuous and often engender reactions in kind. For example, when we react to a child's aggressive behavior, such as biting a peer, by hollering at him or her, we often provoke a reaction in return, such as a startled look, tears, or the child yelling at us. Reactions are not thought-based, and reactive communication is not productive. We need to be thoughtful when speaking with others and/or while doing things, and we must keep impulsivity, reaction, and overreaction to a minimum. We must think before we act and speak so the children learn to do so as well.

As teachers, we do more than we realize when we work with children. We are important to the process because we provide a wealth of information every day. Children learn about the world through our teachings, words, and actions. They watch us to see how to do things and how to act in different situations. They follow our rules, and they listen to what we say. They incorporate our actions, responses, and approaches without even thinking about it. So we should be fully cognizant of what we are demonstrating—that is, what we are doing and saying. We should use reflection when making plans, think before acting and interacting with others, and make good choices. When we are effective role models, children can follow our example.

Once children are aware of what we do, we can make them aware of what they need to do. We should delineate clear expectations so they know what we want from them. We should define rules that they can follow and provide limits to guide their behavior. We should consistently enforce the rules and limits over time, and across situations and children. We should ask children to make good choices everyday, support them when they err, and acknowledge their "good thinking" when they do well. That is the full measure of an excellent preschool teacher.

In conclusion, teachers should maintain a child-centered and child-friendly preschool classroom, and should keep the children's ages and developmental levels in mind when planning. They should offer stimulating materials and provide positive and productive learning opportunities. Teachers should help all children define their interests and assist them in developing their skills. They should present the subject matter and new concepts in personally meaningful ways and make it pertinent to children's life experience. Learning experiences should be kept fun and manageable. Teachers need to define clear expectations and provide firm limits for children, and should teach by good example. Teachers should acknowledge children's prosocial choices, and children's efforts should always be appreciated. Teachers must be positive, supportive, and invested. But most of all, they must be present as the best teacher possible.

3

Supporting Teaching
Practice Through Observation

Observation is the process of carefully watching and listening to a subject, an individual, or a group, and creating a record of what transpires. An observation can be done one time to establish a baseline or numerous times to assess change or progress. Observations can be conducted within a program by its own personnel—that is, a teacher or an administrator, or by trained objective outsiders. Using observation, we can evaluate specific children, teachers, or teaching teams, and assess general classroom dynamics or the effectiveness of a curriculum. Observations can be done to ascertain strengths as well as areas in need of improvement, and can provide information for comparisons between classrooms.

Why should we observe or be observed? The answer is simple—we gain valuable information that can be used at a later point to document the progress of an individual child, teacher, or group, or that can be used as a baseline for making necessary changes in a preschool environment. We can employ observation to highlight areas that require attention, that indicate personally meaningful learning experiences for children and/or underscore strong teaching practice. Objective observations allow us to identify program strengths and weaknesses, formulate action plans, and make changes that enhance a preschool overall.

THE VALUE OF IN-HOUSE OBSERVATION

Some programs make effective use of observation. Classroom teachers might periodically set aside time to informally note the progress of children and/or write out descriptive anecdotes to use during meetings with parents, or they may make more formal assessments of children to identify areas of strength, need, or delay. Teachers might also observe and assess the curriculum as well as the activities that supplement it, to ascertain effectiveness. Lastly, head teachers or center directors may observe and evaluate their own classroom staff for annual reviews.

Directors, education coordinators, and other administrative personnel might also observe and assess the teaching staff and the effectiveness of the curriculum. Often, administrators use evaluative measures to assess the different teaching teams and/or make comparisons between classrooms. Sometimes observations are used as a formal means of data collection.

Observing an Individual Child

Each child is unique, following his or her own personal time frame and developmental path. Even if children are the same age, they are not necessarily at the same developmental point. That is one reason we conduct child-specific observations. They can be used to create individualized education plans, to note developmental changes over time in a given area (e.g., speech or motor development), to document educational progress over a program/school year, or to identify any special needs or delays that might require additional support or intervention. Child observations can range in formality from simple, general, and informal notes on a child's progress or interactions to more formal observations using a standardized measure. Observations can be done directly, with the observer and child in the same area as a standardized test is conducted, or they can be done indirectly, from an observation booth or unobtrusively from a remote point in the classroom.

When we observe a child, we can note his level of cognitive functioning, social skill, vocabulary range, emotional control, and personal style while problem solving and interacting interpersonally. We can appreciate who he is and can develop an individualized lesson plan that will build his skills and offset areas of weakness. By attending to individual children, we can create a context where each can flourish.

Solid adult-child relationships can develop as we discover and appreciate each child's personality and social style. Observing sweet interactive moments and endearing little eccentricities makes children special to us, for these moments define a child and provide a context. From this

---

Point—Observe individual children in various contexts and make notes about the ways each of them acts, reacts, and interacts. By collecting individualized information across learning opportunities and interpersonal relationships, a teacher can assess a child's cognitive and social strengths and weaknesses.

child-specific vantage point, the child's emotional response to different situations can be better understood, and can subsequently provide insight into questionable behaviors or occasional emotional outbursts. Using this knowledge, we can try different approaches to improve relationships or quell problems. When we stop, look, and listen, we learn a great degree about the children we are teaching.

Observing Within a Classroom Setting

Through observation, we can take a "snapshot" of the classroom's daily functioning, of the tone and intensity level of the group, and/or of the quality of the teaching team. General observation yields a wealth of information, such as the nature of the group and its dynamics, the consistency of the teaching team across the program day, and the quality of the educational experience after shift changes. In addition, observational assessment can provide information about the strength of teacher-directed activities, the appeal of the free choice options, and whether or not the curriculum meets the needs of children and provides a solid foundation for learning.

Observing the Dynamics of the Group

When the children are observed en masse, a teacher is able to see and hear the exchanges that take place and can identify which individuals, social pairings, and/or small groups might need extra attention or additional supervision. Children can be assessed as they work, play, and interact, and the teaching team can make adjustments that enhance the social and learning experience.

Based on the information gained from a group observation and the general comparisons that can be made between children within the group, teachers can note areas in a child's experience that need extra work and planning, or can identify developmental or behavioral issues that need further observation and/or support.

Children will be children, and they vary widely in their social skill development. Some children may dominate others and wield tremendous social power in the classroom. In contrast, shy or quiet children may resist participating in large-group gatherings, stay to themselves, or cling to one friend during a group experience. Using observation, teachers can note the dynamics of the group as well as the personal styles of individuals. They can note who is being excluded or bullied, as well as who is wielding the greatest social power, and then make adjustments to restore balance. Difficult pairings can be split up and small-group time can be used to enhance social skills.

Lastly, one can ascertain whether the general tone of a classroom favors learning or detracts from it. A wide range of possibility can be witnessed—some groups are more reserved, quiet, and focused; some groups are loud, energetic, and active; and some groups are out of control, unmanageable, and prone to disruptive outbursts and behavioral issues. An observation can provide insight here. Is the tone related to the teaching style, the room arrangement, the presentation and availability of materials, the physical space, or just a result of the general nature of the children in the group? If the experience is a positive one, what factors contribute to this success and can they be replicated elsewhere? If the experience is negative, what must be changed to make the experience more positive? Sometimes we discover an easy fix (e.g., provide more materials so the children do not have to fight over them or add more sound-absorbing materials to decrease the noise level). Sometimes the solution is more complex (e.g., the teacher is ill-suited to the age range, the group has a number of children with behavioral issues, or the teaching team is out of sync and the children are responding to the lack of consistency). When we can identify the underlying causes for why situations succeed, then we can replicate them; and when they falter, we can make the necessary changes to address them.

Information from a group observation can indicate areas that require further professional development. Perhaps the teaching team would benefit from a workshop on classroom dynamics and management, effective communication, bullying, or the socioemotional development during the preschool period. We can only make adjustments when we note which areas are not up to par or working well.

Observing Teachers and Teaching Teams

Each teaching team can be evaluated throughout the year to see how the grouping meshes and functions. Some teams have longevity and have been together in a classroom or with an age group for years; others are brand new and are just learning how to work together. It is always wise to check on their progress occasionally and give feedback to the staff.

An observation can be done for a single teacher or a team. When the subject is a specific teacher, an assessment can yield valuable information about his or her personal style and/or teaching ability, the effectiveness of his or her communications with the children and other adults, and the manner in which he or she presents materials to the children and follows through with learning opportunities. Furthermore, through observation we can learn whether the teacher is performing as expected in the job as well as whether they fit within the program structure. Lastly, individual teacher observations can show whether there has been progress over time and can help directors determine salary as well as future employment.

From an observation, we can ascertain if the teaching pair or small group is working in concert or is experiencing interpersonal strain. In addition, we can see which areas need support (e.g., interpersonal communication, classroom management, delegation of responsibility) and what areas are strong, and then provide guidance and direction to make the teaching experience fruitful and positive.

Observations conducted before and after shift changes yield a wealth of information that can affect program quality across the day. In day-long programs, a change in staffing usually occurs around the middle of the day, such as during lunch or nap time. Depending on the team, the quality of the education experience can rise, fall, or be maintained when second-shift teachers assume charge of the group. Typically, preschool teachers who begin the day are the more seasoned professionals who work full-time and have extensive knowledge and/or experience in early childhood settings, whereas staff members who end the day are often part-time workers, with less work experience. As a result, sometimes program quality slides from a program that is rich in learning opportunity to one that provides more open-ended care. Administrators should know if the quality changes dramatically, and that information can be determined through observations done throughout the morning and afternoon program hours.

Observations can determine if the quality is maintained across program classrooms as well. Some preschools have multiple classrooms serving a given age group—thus, it is wise to make sure that the educational experience is comparable across classes (e.g., all "fours" classes). Of course, teaching style and personalities will play a large role in classroom dynamics, but putting those variables aside, observations can reveal whether the children are learning similar material in productive ways. Is the curriculum in one room stronger than in another room? What teacher-directed and/or free choice activities are done to support learning? Do the rooms have comparable materials? Are the materials being used effectively? Where does each teacher show his or her particular strength? What are the points of weakness? Does the team as a whole adequately cover all the learning areas and provide an optimal education experience for the children? All this information and more can be determined by sitting quietly, listening, and watching.

From a program-wide standpoint, taking these numerous "snapshots" across the breadth of classroom settings provides a clear image of all the teaching teams. Direct observation will shed light on the varied interpersonal approaches, teaching strategies, lesson plans, and learning activities offered across the groups. Comparing and contrasting the information can lead to the sharing of strengths (effective communication practices, engaging activities, successful strategies for teaching, and so on), which enhance a program across the board, and can provide a starting point for identifying and addressing problems and issues that exist throughout a program.

Observing Adult-Child Interactions

The best way to learn about interactions is to watch and listen to them. An observation provides significant insight into the interpersonal interactions and dynamics within a classroom setting. An observer can see where a teacher fully engages children and where improvements might be made. For example, a teacher might demonstrate outstanding strength when presenting activities to individual children and working one-on-one, but have tremendous difficulty maintaining order when working with a larger group or managing social dynamics between children. Or a teacher might be wonderful at leading a group at circle time or holding the children's attention at story time but have trouble engaging in personal conversations with individual children. Based on observation, we can ascertain a teacher's ability to work in different situations and subsequently support the teacher by either making a change, such as moving him or her to a different age-group level or tweaking a teaching team, or by providing professional development that strengthens his or her skills. Sometimes, just providing direct feedback can assist a teacher in making improvements.

An observer might note discrepancies in a teacher's style, tone, and consistency. For example, a teacher might be particularly firm with one child and then be more malleable with others. The teacher might even have obvious favorites among the children. This simple assessment may provide insight into why some children in the group seem angrier than others, as well as why some children seem to have greater power over their peers. Since children can observe dynamics as well as adults do, they can see inequities (e.g., favoritism, unequal treatment) and react to it, or they may feel empowered as the perceived "favorite" and lord it over others. The adult-child dynamic can dramatically shape peer relationships, intentionally or unintentionally.

Observing Teacher Practice

Over the course of a day, teachers perform a variety of tasks and execute a number of routines. The daily schedule outlines the course of the day and highlights the periods designated for learning and/or play, as well as the various routines that the group will experience, such as meal time, nap time, and diapering/toileting.

Teacher performance can be evaluated across all the varied points of the day to assess strengths and weaknesses. Although a great deal of focus is often placed on the implementation of curriculum, the successful presentation of materials, the introduction of conceptual information, and the quality of teaching and adult-child interactions, staff performance and adherence to standards as the teachers carry out daily routines is equally as important.

Observational assessment can span a broad range. We can learn about the specific abilities of teachers across conceptual areas (e.g., math, science, literacy, language development) and assess their competence, and we can determine a teacher's strength or weakness in facilitating social and emotional development (e.g., helping children adjust to the environment, integrating them into group situations, supporting them when they are upset). We can evaluate a teacher's ability to impart information in a fun and meaningful way. We can assess his or her attention to detail when completing chores and daily routines. Regardless of the task at hand, through observation, we can determine the level of commitment teachers have for the job, the extent to which they are invested in the children, the amount of care they show when presenting the curriculum, and the degree to which they meet the health, safety, and cleanliness standards set forth by the program.

Observing the Curriculum in Action

Preschool curricula vary greatly in their methodology and content. There are prepackaged early childhood education curricula that are specific to subjects, such as math, science, and literacy, and there are others that take a broader and more encompassing approach to learning. Some curricula focus on the socioemotional realm and address interpersonal growth and development as their main goal. Others are purely academic and define success through skill acquisition, cognitive advancement, and achievement. Some are theme-based and follow a specific calendar; others are emergent and subject to change based on the children's interests. Some curricula demand conformity and leave little room for teaching style; others are very loose and allow for a great deal of variety across classrooms.

Regardless of the actual content, the most important aspect of a curriculum is whether it interests, supports, and enhances the learning experience of children. Does it accomplish what it sets out to do? Does it engage children and lead to valuable learning?

When observing a curriculum in action, the goal is to see whether the educational program fits the learning environment and benefits the children. Is it age-appropriate and developmentally attuned to the group? That is, does it address the physical, emotional, cognitive, and social abilities of young children and support change in these areas over time? Is the content interesting and engaging? Are the activities offered fun and stimulating, and do they hold a child's attention? Is the program child-friendly, or is it more adult-driven? Does it offer direct learning with hands-on opportunities for discovery and exploration, or is it mostly teacher-directed and rote-based teaching? How successful is its implementation? In what ways can we gauge success? The answer to these questions will determine the success of the curriculum.

While watching the program in action, it is important to note how often the children can initiate learning on their own and compare that to how often teachers control or dominate learning situations. We should note the level of success experienced by different children in the group. Are the needs of all the children being met? Are the teachers effectively using materials and providing strong learning opportunities? We need to assess the appeal of the materials and the degree to which children participate in various activities. Are the concepts being presented in child-friendly and meaningful ways so each child can learn and feel empowered?

Observing the Classroom Environment

The preschool classroom can be an ally or an enemy. Many teachers do not factor in the impact of the space when assessing learning outcomes, yet it can play a major role in a group's success or failure. The physical makeup of the space, the arrangement of the furnishings, the placement of the centers, and the general feeling of the room can impact the day-to-day results. Observe the environment, note the problems or issues, and address them so they no longer affect the early learning experience.

An objective observation of the space can identify the numerous minor irritations and infractions that cumulatively affect learning. Begin with the sensory experience of the space—that is, the temperature, the amount of light, the sound level, and the presence of distinct odors. Is the room temperature too hot, too cold, or just right? Is the air refreshing or stale? Is the level of brightness consistent throughout the room? Can the amount of natural light be controlled? Do the uncovered windows make the space hot? Are sounds effectively buffered, or is the space too loud and overwhelming? Are there any unpleasant odors present (e.g., diapers, mildew, mustiness)?

Next, note the initial overall impression of the space. Some programs have barely any items displayed on the walls; others are overloaded with artwork and learning tools. Does the space feel overwhelming? Does it seem flat and unappealing? Does it feel welcoming? Think about the space from the perspective of the children. Would the display be too much for a child—too colorful, too bold, overstimulating, or chaotic? Or does it seem unfriendly, stark, empty, or boring?

What does the room feel like? Is it child-friendly or child-oriented? Is it old and worn out, or fresh and new? Is it inviting, dirty, organized, cozy, boring? Would a child feel safe here? Does it embrace diversity and welcome all families?

Is the space crowded with furniture, too small and cramped, too wide-open, or arranged in a child-friendly manner? What centers are available, and are they well-stocked? Can children easily access materials or are the shelves overloaded? Are the children engaged in active play in all areas? Does the size of each center adequately accommodate the number of children playing there? Is there a space set aside for privacy or quiet time for a single child? Are quiet centers separated from the more active ones? Are the furnishings sized correctly for the children in the group? Are there enough chairs, cots, and materials for the number of children in the class? By taking the time to really assess the space, we can see how it can affect the classroom dynamic and the quality and amount of learning that occurs within it.

In conclusion, observational assessments conducted in-house by teaching and administrative staff members can supply a great deal of information about the performance of individual children, specific teachers, and teaching teams, as well as adult-adult and adult-child interactions. Furthermore, observations yield data on the effectiveness of curricula, on the functioning of a certain classroom or on an entire age-specific stratum (e.g., 3-year-olds), provide comparison points between classrooms or groups, and assess a preschool or program's quality overall.

THE VALUE OF OBJECTIVE OBSERVATIONS

Although a great deal can be gained from conducting in-house observations, there is also a definite advantage to having an outside observer visit a preschool program and provide objective feedback. Outside observers are unencumbered by the internal relationships and politics that exist within programs, and they are trained to identify strengths, weaknesses, and areas that are in need of improvement. They bring fresh eyes and ears to each classroom they visit.

Utilizing Outside Experts to Make Observations

The advantages of having an objective observation are numerous. For instance, teachers and directors often focus their attention on day-to-day situations and the overall picture, and thus lose sight of small infractions, simple repairs, and general areas that are in need of attention. An independent rater is hired to see the forest as well as the trees, and thus will observe and report on the larger program dimensions (e.g., teaching practice, curriculum, group dynamics, classroom environment) as well as document minor details (e.g., broken furniture, poorly executed routines, specific teacher-child interactions) so proper attention can be paid to them.

In addition, friendships and work relationships can interfere with an observer making an objective assessment, resulting in a skewed evaluation. Independent observers have no direct allegiances to staff members and can provide unbiased information on interpersonal interaction, classroom dynamics, the effectiveness of the teaching team, and the overall quality of the teaching and implementation of curriculum.

Outside observers come to the job with an expertise that qualifies them for the work they do. Many are trained in the implementation of specific assessment measures and have reached a level of reliability that ensures that they are giving accurate information to the program. Being well-versed in the measure and having experience using it enables objective outsiders to make solid statements about the subjects they are observing.

Observing Classroom Environments Using Standardized Measures

A number of standardized assessments measures have been created to assist in determining the quality of preschool classrooms. Some examine specific aspects of a classroom environment, such as the *Early Language and Literacy Classroom Observation* or ELLCO (Smith & Dickinson, 2002); others, like the *Early Childhood Environment Rating Scale–Revised edition* (ECERS–R) (Harms, Clifford, & Cryer, 2005), assess the preschool experience by focusing on a variety of features, which directly or indirectly affect a child's ability to develop and learn in the classroom/program environment.

Many programs use the ECERS and/or the ELLCO to get observational feedback, ascertain the quality of a classroom environment, and define specific areas for program improvement. By using these quantitative measures, programs can focus on concrete goals and ascertain whether observable and quantifiable improvements have resulted.

After a standardized assessment has been conducted, it is easy to define a plan for professional development because the report details areas of strength as well as areas in need of improvement. Numerous workshops and/or seminars are available to support teachers in every area of the classroom and across all interpersonal situations. In addition, programs can hire knowledgeable professionals who can provide specific coaching in the areas defined by the observation's report. Thus, having the information is the first step toward program enhancement.

Benefiting Personally from the Observation Process

Regardless of who is the actual observer, we should make sure to benefit from the process as much as possible. Become an observer, and become familiar with a variety of observational assessments. Ask the program administration to purchase a copy of different measures and use them in the classroom. Remove the "teacher" hat and put on the "observer" hat, and see what goes unnoticed on a daily basis and then make improvements.

Stop, look, and listen. Much can be gained from this process. When we are trained to make observations, our perspective is permanently reshaped. We readily attend to details. We learn to quickly identify areas that need improvement and develop a sharpened eye, noting objects that need to be fixed or situations that need to be addressed. We pay greater attention to the social environment and can almost anticipate when things are about to swirl out of control.

By learning to observe, we come to appreciate every aspect of our job more, and we see how everything is connected and interrelated. We realize that making a simple change in one area can cause changes to ripple throughout other areas. We *want* to make changes and improvements because we can see how one simple action can impact in the environment. For example, by adding more materials to a center, we reduce grabbing and fighting; by removing the broken chair, we safeguard a child from injury; by washing our hands and promoting hygiene, we maintain a healthier classroom. Learning to observe and learning from our observations makes us better teachers.

I can personally attest to this. When I was a preschool teacher, I believed that I did a good job. But once I formally learned to do observational assessments, I realized that I could have done even better. By adopting an observer's perspective, my understanding of and appreciation for the job of preschool teacher has grown exponentially.

THE MOST IMPORTANT OBSERVERS

Observations can be done by teachers within their own classroom, by in-house colleagues, and by outside observers. When teachers know they are going to be observed, they take out their best toys and plan special projects. They want to dazzle the observer with great things *this one day*; then return to the regular routine afterward. Unfortunately, teachers incorrectly believe that only adult observers are important. As a result, they demonstrate their highest level of practice when someone comes in to observe or evaluate their performance. Teachers need to remember that they are being observed every day, and they have to appreciate that the observers who count most are the *children*.

Children watch our every move and hear our every word. They learn about the world through our actions, so they are very attentive to our example. All teachers need to be aware of this and meet high standards in behavior in order to be of maximum benefit to them. Children will indicate through their questions and comments when they see discrepancies. For instance, a child might ask why one teacher puts on gloves to prepare lunch but another does not, why a teacher is bringing the first aid bag out to the playground (indicating it does not always come outside), or why they are walking in the lines (e.g., the crosswalk) and not just going directly to the space, suggesting that this practice is not typical. These innocent and enlightening questions clearly show us that the children are paying attention to our practice and noting inconsistencies. We can use this information and be aware of how our actions affect the group, so that best practice can be done consistently.

Small changes in a teacher's level of investment can yield dramatic results in the children's enthusiasm for learning. For example, on one occasion, a teacher was "on," joking with the children and being very funny. All the children were enjoying her, but there was one child in particular who was responding very well. He followed her around the room and giggled the whole morning. One could see from the reaction of his peers that his enthusiasm and level of participation were definitely different this day. After 3 hours, the little boy blurted out, "Miss -----, you've never been this funny before! I like this, can we do this every day?" Although the teacher was performing for the observer, she was a smash hit with the children. Hopefully, her new routine would have a long run to a sell-out audience.

Teachers should work hard to please the children, because happy children hold the ultimate power. When a child goes home and talks about his or her great teacher and about the fun they have at preschool, it directly impacts the program. Happy children yield satisfied parents, which prompts them to speak well of the program, support the classroom staff, and stay with the program in the future. Thus, teachers should prepare for each and every day as if they are having an observation conducted—because they are.

4

Facilitating the Children's Preschool Experience Through Awareness

Awareness is key to successful teaching. We should be aware of our personal attitudes and opinions, as well as our emotions, because they might unconsciously influence our communications and actions. We need to be aware of interpersonal interactions and see how our choices may be impacting our relationships with the children, their parents, and our co-workers. Furthermore, we need to be aware of the typical issues that will emerge in the classroom, such as children's difficulty separating from a parent or making transitions, and of the different strategies and approaches we will need to access when they inevitably arise. We need to be aware of the individual children in our group, their personal needs and interpersonal requirements, and the helpful hints parents use when their child is upset or stressed. Finally, we need to be aware of our own daily practice, periodically review what we are doing, make proactive changes, and then consciously implement new strategies and approaches. When we are fully aware of the full context of our job, the children, and where we fit into the picture, we are able to do exemplary work.

KNOWING WHAT AFFECTS TEACHER-CHILD RELATIONSHIPS

People do not exist in a vacuum. We affect one another. Our thoughts, words, and actions are broadcast outward through our verbal and nonverbal communication, and they impact every person in the immediate environment. Since the process is reciprocal, we are in turn impacted by others.

Our Attitudes Have Power

Attitude is *everything*! If we have a positive attitude, we make a certain kind of choice consistently. Our outlook is shaped by the way we view things and by how we choose to interpret the actions of others. If we have a negative view, we act in entirely different ways. We may refrain from completing tasks or involving ourselves with others because we have poor expectations for the outcome.

We actively choose our attitudes about life, every minute of every day. They shape our routines, our perceptions, and our relationships. Our attitudes can be affected by the silliest things, such as the weather, or by major life-changing events, such as a loss. Once attitudes are formed, it takes a lot to replace or reshape them.

How we perceive the world correlates with how we respond to it. Think of the saying "the glass is half-empty, the glass is half-full." Seeing the glass as having more will have a different outcome in our thoughts, feelings, and actions from seeing the glass as not having a lot. Optimism makes work seem easier and makes the load life hands us seem lighter. Pessimism creates a feeling of indifference, disinterest, or outright disgust. In order to cope well with the tasks and trials we encounter, it is better to opt for optimism.

By realizing that our attitudes have power, we can alter our experiences and have a better time when we are with children. We should consider our attitudes toward the job, the children, the parents, and co-workers, and strive to have a positive outlook to ensure success.

Our Emotions Are Influential

Early childhood educators must realize that our emotions affect children. Infants, toddlers, and preschoolers adeptly read our level of stress by looking at our faces—and inevitably, they react to it. If we are having a bad day, we have to check it at the door when we come to work. Otherwise, we can guarantee ourselves an even worse day.

Young children can read our emotional tone and know whether we are having a bad day just by looking at us. This directly affects their sense of security. They react negatively to people when they feel stressed by them, and they react positively when they feel comfortable. Since young children are keenly aware of the emotional messages we are relaying, we should be, too.

When we are calm and in control of our thoughts and emotions, we can better assist children in making successful adjustments. When we are not calm, we unwittingly contribute to the problem and create more tension. When children feel our stress, they become more stressed, which creates an unpleasant cycle for all. We must be aware of and accountable for our social cues in order to be effective teachers.

KNOWING WHAT IS LIKELY TO HAPPEN, DEVELOPMENTALLY

Knowing and anticipating the typical struggles that young children experience as they develop, such as stranger anxiety, separation difficulties, and transition troubles, can prepare us so we can better assist them in their adjustment. We must keep in mind, however, that the severity of the expressed problem is totally dependent upon the child. Individual differences play a huge role, so respecting, appreciating, and understanding each child as an individual will make the adjustment process much easier.

Anticipating Separation Issues in Young Children

Separation anxiety or intense emotionality in the form of crying, withdrawing, and/or refusing to participate results from being separated from a significant "other" or placed in an unfamiliar environment. This can be very disruptive to a child's sense of well-being. Although we may want to, we can't *make* a child separate; we can only support him or her through the process. Separation anxiety must run its natural course in order to be resolved. Therefore, we need to take our cues from the child's level of anxiety and provide emotional and social support.

When I think back to the first day school for my "Twos," I clearly remember how hard it was for the children and their parents to separate. Three mothers had real trouble leaving, making it all the more difficult for their children. Since the mothers were unwilling to depart, the children sensed their reluctance and clung to them more tightly, which reinforced the mothers' maternal concern. A vicious cycle began. The longer it went on, the worse it got, until even those children who had successfully separated began to react to the strain of the moment. Once the mothers all left, my coworkers and I had 10 2-year-olds standing by the doors and windows in tears. *Everyone* needed loving support, including us teachers! Yet, by keeping level heads and giving comforting hugs, we helped the children slowly begin to trust us and feel safe in our care. We just needed to be in control of our own emotions so we did not add to the stress. We needed to be good role models.

Point—We must show the children through our words and actions that grown-ups are people to trust, respect, and turn to for support and assistance.

> **Point**—We must remember that children look to us for information and example. As teachers, we do more than impart information about content material; we also model how to be people.

We should get to know each child and his or her unique needs and meet them quickly so the overall tone of the relationship remains positive. It is easier to entertain a happy child than it is to console an upset one. We can anticipate meltdowns by attending to cues so problems can be avoided or intercepted. This will make the whole adjustment process easier.

During separations, we should support the child throughout the exchange and help him or her feel safe and secure. Do not remove "loveys" (e.g., pacifiers, blankies) at this time, because children need these things to provide security when they are stressed. Give positive messages to everyone involved—the child, the parent, and the other children in the group—and redirect the child's attention as soon as possible. Provide comfort and hold the child until he or she relaxes and feels secure.

Awareness Is Crucial When Making Transitions

Separation is the physical act of leaving someone, whereas transition is a psychological state, and may require more work. Transitions occur all day: when arriving in the morning, between activities, when leaving for home, at key points in the daily routine (e.g., mealtime, naptime, waking up from a nap, diapering/toileting), and we must be prepared for them. Provide ample time and be positive. Stay calm and give everyone enough time to adjust; don't raise the level of anxiety by rushing. Stay in control. Refrain from engaging in power struggles, which reduce everyone to the age of the youngest person involved.

Be clear, predictable, and straightforward. Stick to the plan to avoid confusing the situation. Confusion breeds anxiety. Explain things *briefly* and in advance. Give the group warnings (e.g., "2 minutes until clean-up!") so the transition does not sneak up on them. Finally, encourage language and help children find words so they can ask for help or express their wants and needs to others. Give them the words that get results.

Get Child-Specific Information from Parents

When a child joins a group, it is always helpful to get a history that can provide insight into that child and his or her needs. Ask the parent questions about daily routines, the child's sleep history, feeding needs, diapering and/or toileting requirements, and so forth. Getting this infor-

> **Point**—Ask for family photos before the first day, then laminate the pictures and place them on a closeable ring (rather than on the classroom wall). This way, a child can carry around the ring and flip through the pictures when he or she needs "family" time.

mation gives us an idea of how the child adapts to routines, and whether he or she is high- or low-maintenance.

In addition, ask about family members, siblings, pets, and other special objects. This provides a frame of reference if the child mentions these things during the day. Children get very frustrated when they want to share information with us, such as "I like my Fluffy," and we have no clue what they mean. Unless we already know that Fluffy is a pet gerbil, we might think it is a cat, dog, stuffed animal, or security blanket.

Ask for any "tricks" that the parents use to soothe or engage the child. Request a personal item that smells like Mommy, such as a hairbrush or scarf, to have on hand as a "security object" for when the child misses her. Finally, request photos of loved ones, so the child can touch or hold them when he or she feels homesick.

Remembering the Importance of Attachment

Attachment is an emotional bond between people that provides a sense of deep connection and security. Children need to feel secure in order to thrive. This underlying social bond can make a child feel safe and secure, or it can have a negative impact and lead to social and behavioral issues. Children show their level of attachment to others through many of their social behaviors, including their need to maintain close proximity, through smiling, making eye contact, calling out to a person across a room, touching, clinging, and/or crying. Ultimately, we want to create successful relationships with each child so he or she feels safe and secure with us.

Preschool teachers should bond with each child and be committed to forming a relationship with him or her by being consistent and caring over time and across situations. We should develop a rapport with each child by talking with him or her about personal situations that make him or her feel special. We should acknowledge each child's uniqueness and respond to it with positive regard, engage him or her with gentleness, and assist him or her in defining a positive sense of self by acknowledging accomplishments (e.g., physically, socially, and cognitively).

Lastly, we need to create a positive and constructive social environment where all children feel supported and protected, are respected, and are treated with fairness, kindness, and compassion. It is vital that all children feel valued, for it is at this point in their development that they deem themselves either worthy or worthless, and shape their impressions about school and their place within it.

KNOWING WHAT IS IN THE ENVIRONMENT—USE A DISCERNING EYE

Preschool programs should provide a safe and healthy place for children to learn and play. All adults in the environment are responsible for its up-keep and cleanliness, so we need to routinely check all areas that children can access.

Since subsequent chapters will examine health and safety routines and practices in greater depth, we will focus on just a few points regarding common spaces and general classroom safety here.

Awareness of the Environment—Keeping Children Safe

On any given day, our attention as teachers is focused on the individual children, the overall group dynamics, and the learning opportunities. Our attention is not always dedicated to the environment, but it should be. We need to find those areas that might be detrimental to children and address them before the children find them and get hurt.

Consider the whole building when making an assessment of its safety. Look in the parking lot for stray pieces of broken glass or cigarette butts and remove them. Is the front entrance secure, or can a child easily leave the safety of the building? In the common hallways, are all of the outlets covered? Are the floors and baseboards hastily cleaned? Is the space cluttered with unused furniture and equipment? A lot can be learned about a program by walking down a hallway.

Preschool Classroom—Ally or Enemy?

Every classroom has a few things that need tweaking. That is normal. Despite our best efforts, no environment is perfect. Carefully attend to the classroom environment, making sure it is child-safe. Specifically, examine those places that have been overlooked but could lead to serious injury or worse if left unattended.

Observe the space from varied angles and areas. Look around while standing up, while sitting in a chair, and while seated on the floor. What can be seen from this level? What cannot be seen? This is very important because there are some spaces that are obscured from direct view when situated lower to the ground. Although teachers assert that they move around the room and/or station themselves so they can see, we have to

> **Point**—Avoid creating obscure nooks that prevent easy visual supervision from various points in the room. If a child does not want to be seen, he or she may be up to something. After all, they are children.

be sure that when we are seated on the floor or at a table we can see *all* the children at any time.

Consider this example. A "Threes" group, consisting of 18 children and two teachers, was enjoying free play in an L-shaped classroom. The teachers were working with the majority of the group in one area of the room. The book nook was located in the far corner and had cozy, soft cushions and a slanted bookcase that divided it from the main classroom space. The teacher created a little nook between the wall and the bookshelf for privacy; however, children who were seated there were not fully visible from much of the room.

A hungry child grabbed a few Saltine packs from the snack shelf and went to the book nook. No staff member noticed. He voraciously stuffed the crackers into his mouth. As the crackers dried up the moisture in his mouth and throat and became gluey, he began to choke. Since he was hiding, no one knew he was in distress. Had someone not noticed what was happening, the child might have choked to death. It only takes a moment for a good day to turn bad. Teachers should always know where every child is, what the children are doing, and should be able to see them in a split second—just in case.

One solution to supervising children visually in problem areas is to install mirrors in the ceiling corners, so teachers can glance up every now and again and see if anyone is in a hard-to-see area. Such mirrors may seem costly, by some programs' standards, but in the end, they are always worth the money if they prevent loss of life.

Search the space for the location of items that might be needed in an emergency, such as the first aid kit, the telephone for outside calls, and attendance sheets and emergency contact information cards. Is the first aid kit in plain view? If not, put a big red cross over its location, so it is clearly marked. Is there a phone in the room, and can it be used to make outside calls? All classrooms should have an outside line as well as an in-house intercom so vital communication is not delayed. Lastly, where

> **Point**—Privacy spaces should be easy to see into from different points in the room. If a little tent or a curtained-off space is provided for privacy, be sure that children are visible.

> **Point**—Post your emergency exit plan by each classroom door. Post your emergency evacuation plans in the classroom and in the hall for everyone to see.

is the emergency information (e.g., emergency contact cards, attendance sheets, and evacuation plans for fire and other emergency situations)? Are emergency plans posted? Is child-specific information gathered in one place for immediate access? In an emergency, time should not be lost trying to find attendance sheets or phone numbers.

Make a point to scan the classroom every day for hazards such as loose electrical cords. Think of little feet for a moment. Young children do not pay attention to their feet as they move around. How many seem to trip over air? How likely is it, then, that a foot could get tangled in a loose cord? I have seen many computer centers with cords dangling down the back of the table, or worse, left underfoot. When children slide chairs in and out of the desk space, how many times do they land on the wire? Frayed wires can cause fires. Secure the wires to the wall, furnishings, or the floor so they don't move or get crushed.

Are electrical cords from music players hanging in the children's active play space (e.g., the dramatic play area or the block corner)? What would happen if a child intentionally or inadvertently pulled on the cord while playing and the music player fell off the shelf? It has happened, and children have been hurt. To avoid such incidents, affix cords to the furniture, floor, or wall with Velcro strips so no child can get hurt.

Note where there are open outlets such as on the walls or in bathroom spaces. Cover them. Avoid using power strips when possible, but when they are used, limit the number and cover all open outlets. Curious hands could be in danger. Don't use extension cords. They can fray, become tripping hazards, or can come loose, leaving an open and direct electrical connection.

Children will be children. They are very curious little people and they often get into places where they should not be. It is our job to keep them safe. Be sure to store items that could be dangerous to young children on a high shelf or in locked areas so they are out of reach. Lock away personal items, such as purses and tote bags, so children cannot access them. This is especially important if these bags contain medication, cigarettes, or sharp objects.

> **Point**—Cover all unused outlets wherever children play or go (e.g., bathrooms, central hallways). Secure all power cords to the floor or wall to prevent tripping or accidental pulls.

Any chemicals that are used for cleaning should be kept in high, closed cabinets or in lockable containers. In addition, medication for specific children should be kept in a secure place.

It is always nice to have plants in the classroom for aesthetic purposes and to clean the air. Make sure the plants are nontoxic and nonpoisonous. If they require chemicals for their care, such as fertilizer or pesticides, keep these items locked away.

Lastly, make sure that all paints and glue products are child-friendly as well.

Walk around the room and inspect the walls and floors. Look for peeling paint and clean it up. Make sure it is not lead-based, and if it is, sand away points where it is blistering, then thoroughly vacuum the area and repaint the space with a latex paint, if necessary. Move furniture and look under heating vents and along baseboards for evidence of pests in the room (e.g., insects or vermin). If these are present, attend to them immediately.

During a general review of the space, make sure rugs and carpets are tacked down so no one trips. Place rubber backing on throw rugs so they do not cause a slip-and-fall accident. If there are any exposed nails or screws with lifted heads, hammer or screw them down so they are flush with the surface. Put all sharp scissors and sharp objects in a container that is out of the children's reach. Get on the floor and look for small items that might choke children or be ingested, such as spent staples, small beads, and thumbtacks. Pop into the bathroom, take a deep breath, and see if it looks and smells clean.

Note what is stored on the top of shelf units. Consider the following example when placing objects there. A teacher set aside a "cozy" space between two 30-inch-high shelf units. She placed soft cushions there as well as books and materials for quiet play. It looked ideal—except for the wooden box perched on top of one of the shelf units, containing 10 or 12 puzzles. Though the box was heavy with puzzles, it could move when the right amount of force was applied.

A small child was sitting contentedly in this U-shaped nook, looking at a book. Two rambunctious children ran by and knocked into the shelf unit, sending the puzzle box flying off the edge. The box landed with a thud and a scream. Luckily, it fell into an open space and not on the little girl who was sitting there. If it had hit her, she would have sustained a serious injury.

> **Point**—Store all toxic liquids (e.g., bleach, cleaning solutions) in closed and locked cabinets. Place only nontoxic and nonpoisonous plants in the room. Keep purses or personal items and any medication in locked closets or cabinets.

> **Point**—Bump into furniture to see if it wobbles or is unsteady. Remove any items on top of shelf units or windowsills that might fall and potentially injure children.

Are items stored on top of the shelf units and windowsills? Could something fall off if it were knocked or pulled? It doesn't take much to make a child trip and fall. They do it every day. Move any items that might fall so no one gets hurt.

How about the furnishings (e.g., shelf units, easels, dramatic play props, freestanding cabinets)? Are they sturdy or wobbly? If a child fell into them, would they topple over? Are furnishings secured to the wall or floor to prevent movement? What shape are they in? Run an open hand across the wood and note whether they require sanding, repainting, or replacement, or whether they are in poor shape and need to be cleaned, upgraded, or discarded.

Now consider the tables and chairs that are used by the children daily. Do they fit the size of the children? Many times, chairs are too big for the children; as a result, they sit far forward in order to reach the floor. Since small children have a high center of gravity, they often topple forward, lose their balance, and fall. Thus, the chairs should fit the children, and when fully seated, a child should be able to touch the floor. If children's feet dangle, they are not safe if they shift their weight. Are the chairs balanced, or are they missing stabilizing feet? Are the seats broken or splintered? Do the chairs have pinch points that might catch or puncture skin? Would we feel safe sitting on them?

How about the tables? Are they the right height for the children when they are seated in their chairs? Adjust them so the table edge comes midway up the children's torso, so they can rest their elbows comfortably on the tabletop when seated. If their little chins line up with the table edge, lower it. This height may be uncomfortable for the teacher, but remember the student–teacher ratio. There are more of them, so they win.

Are the tables sturdy or wobbly? Balance them so they don't tilt when weight is applied. Children have enough trouble learning to write their numbers and letters on firm surfaces. Why complicate the process with uneven table legs?

> **Point**—Remove any furniture that is in disrepair. Adjust the tables so they are level. Place old tennis balls on any chairs that are missing balancing feet to make them stable.

Indoor Gross-Motor Areas

Make a thorough inspection of the indoor gross-motor space and make sure it meets high safety standards. If it is a gym space, peruse the walls and cover all outlets. Check that each lighting fixture is firmly attached and protected in the event that an errant ball hits it. If the space is a converted classroom or a large common hall space, look for hazards and address them.

Check the equipment to see that it is in good repair. Look for broken plastic and either repair it or remove the item. If riding toys or tricycles are used, check their size and see if they fit the children in the group. Have the children wear helmets so they are less likely to sustain a head injury if they fall or crash. Be proactive and attentive to the space and equipment so you can focus on the actions of the children as they engage in active play.

Determining Playground Safety

How safe is the playground? It could be the standard bearer or the bane of a program's existence. So much requires attention; teachers must be alert.

Let's start with the general safety of the outdoor space. Is the onsite outdoor play space fenced? Must the children cross streets or parking lots to get to the playground? If offsite, is the public park safe? How far away from the building do the children walk? What hazards might they encounter?

Playgrounds come in all shapes and sizes, and each has its own set of high points and low points. For example, one playground I visited was so far from the building that the children got a full day's worth of exercise just going to it. We literally had to cross a parking lot, go down a set of cement stairs, cross through a thicket of trees, go by bridge over a small stream, and then walk around the exterior of a fence to enter through a gate. I thought the trip was far for a group of 3-year-olds, but they proved me wrong. Once there, they wildly raced around the space. I guess it was just long for *me*. To my relief, the teacher carried out a first aid kit and a walkie-talkie for emergencies. It would have been difficult to get everyone back quickly and safely had a child become ill or injured.

If the preschool program has an onsite playground space, does a fence keep the children in and unwanted visitors out? Are there trash or other risky items (e.g., broken glass, half-smoked cigarette butts) that need to be removed before the children enter? Is the gross-motor equipment in good shape, or does it require repair or replacement (e.g., rusty metal, splintered wood, broken equipment, rusty or exposed nails)? Is the equipment (e.g., climber, swings, slides) sized correctly for the children? Would the existing cushioning beneath the climber sufficiently safeguard children and prevent injury?

> **Point**—There should be at least 8 inches of soft surfacing or cushioning (sand, wood chips, etc.) around climbers, swings, and slides to reduce impact injuries.

One program had a playground adjacent to the building so the children had a short walk to it. There were many toys and a variety of climbing equipment contained within the fenced-in space. The parking lot, though not fenced in, was cordoned off with cones and used for tricycles and riding toys, which seemed harmless, except for the precipitous 10-foot drop at the far end. To prevent accidents, a teacher stationed herself there to monitor the bike riders. At first, it seemed manageable, but as the number of children riding bikes increased, it became more and more difficult to keep track of them. I just kept anticipating one child riding over the edge and no one knowing it for a while, if at all.

How about the space for running, jumping, and climbing? Can the children get hit by passing swings? How much space surrounds the equipment to prevent injury? For each climber, slide, or swing, a minimum of 6 feet of space must be set aside as a fall zone. For a swing, there must be at least 6 feet on each side of the swing set, front and back. If two pieces of equipment are placed next to each other (e.g., a climber and slide) there must be 12 feet of space separating them, 6 feet for each item.

What about areas for potential entrapment? Are there spaces large enough for a little head to get stuck, perhaps between posts in a railing or under climbing surfaces? If so, place a barrier over the space so children cannot get trapped.

Consider this scenario. A teacher frequently pushed unused climbing equipment over to the side of the play yard, near a chain-link fence. This practice seemed harmless. One day, two little boys climbed onto this unused equipment and pretended to be swashbuckling pirates. When two other boys came to join them, the first pair tried to jump off and run away. One of the boys just barely missed getting his jacket hood snagged on the fence post. Had his feet been centimeters closer to the fence, he would have been hanged. Once alerted to this, the teachers moved the climber away from the fence, creating a narrow alley, not the required 6 feet of space. On a subsequent visit, I noted that all the equipment was pushed along the fence. Accident averted—lesson unlearned.

> **Point**—There should be at least a 6-foot fall zone of clear space around all climbing structures or equipment on the playground.

> **Point**—Look for potential entrapment points. Measure the space between handrails, at the bottom of the slides, under the climbing structure, between fence posts and gates, and under fencing. If a large grapefruit can fit through it, it needs to be fixed.

What about the paved surfaces? Do they provide good footing? Is the surface a continuous grade? Is it level? Can a child run on it without tripping? Or is it made up of broken concrete and/or patched cement? Are the seams lifted and likely to trip a child? Are roots under the surface lifting and cracking the cement? Can children easily ride their tricycles on it? Do the tricycle riders wear protective helmets?

What about the grassy areas? Can a child trip when crossing it? Are there holes that can catch a foot or twist an ankle? Are there hidden curbs or steps, or uneven drainage grates?

> **Point**—Check the playground space before the children enter it. Always clear it of trash, dirty diapers, broken glass, and hazardous materials (drug paraphernalia, used condoms).

Offsite Play Areas

Many urban programs use public parks for gross-motor activity, and children walk along streets with speeding cars and/or broken sidewalks covered with shards of glass and trash. A lot can go wrong in a short time. Teachers must be especially attentive while out in public with children.

For example, one time, I walked with a group of children bound for some outdoor fun. The distance they traveled shocked me; they walked nearly three-quarters of a mile each way to a neighborhood park on a humid 90-degree day. Unfortunately, the teachers did not bring any water with them, so after the one-way walk, the children were hot and miserable. The locked bathrooms at the park made things worse. One child wet himself because he forgot to use the bathroom before leaving the preschool and could not hold it for the whole walk. Always plan for the worst and hope for the best when leaving the preschool premises.

> **Point**—If children must cross a parking lot or street to get to the playground, always use crosswalks. Be aware of trip points on the pavement. A seam or crack can lead to stumbles. Point them out so no one trips.

Always anticipate what might be encountered and prepare for it in advance. We might meet just about anything or anyone while at a public park (e.g., unsavory people, unfamiliar animals such as dogs or ferrets, questionable objects), which makes me question whether sufficient contingency plans may even exist. For instance, does the teacher have a cell phone or another way to contact someone for help if a situation takes a turn for the worse (e.g., a child suffers a dog bite, a child wanders away from the group, a menacing adult approaches)? What precautions can be taken if the space proves to be unsafe (e.g., has broken glass, garbage, needles, half-smoked cigarette butts, condoms, crack pipes)? What can be done if a child wanders off or goes out of sight? How can help be summoned if a child is injured, gets sick, or becomes unruly and out of control? When on the playground with young children, we have to be ready for anything and prepared for everything.

Accommodating Everyone

Federal law mandates that all children, including those with disabilities, have access to an equal education. Every child should feel welcomed and be included in the daily routine, as should their family members.

How attentive is the preschool to the needs of people with handicapping conditions? Is there a ramp or elevator to make the space handicapped-accessible? Can doors and bathrooms accommodate wheelchairs? Do the doors have grip handles or standard doorknobs?

Children with physical disabilities have enough to manage. Make the space easily accessible, not just because of the law, but because it is the right thing to do. Open the door frames to 36 inches so that a wheelchair can pass through. Have a handicapped-accessible bathroom available so that a child or adult can use it without incident. Have tables that can accommodate a wheelchair so a child can remain with the group and be a part of the activity.

Once, I observed a program that was very sensitive to people in wheelchairs . . . or so the program staff believed. They installed an elevator to access upstairs classrooms and added a handicapped-accessible entrance ramp at the rear of the building, with a wide concrete path leading to it for wheelchairs. A high fence separated the rear of the building from the handicapped-friendly parking lot. Yet, there was one problem—the locking mechanism for the gate was located at the top of a 6-foot-high pillar. How could a person in a wheelchair reach it? Sometimes it really helps to "ride a mile in someone else's chair."

The few minutes it takes to note and correct these points and infractions can make all the difference in the world.

Now let's move into the classroom.

Part II

THE EARLY CHILDHOOD EDUCATION CLASSROOM PROCESS:

Daily Routines, Practices, and Materials

5

Ensuring a Safe, Healthy, and Happy Classroom

Parents want to place their children in safe, secure, high-quality class-rooms. At minimum, the teachers should be in the proper adult-child ratio, involved in what is happening around them; attentive to the children and their interactions, proactive in removing broken furniture or materials, alert to dangerous situations, and invested in maintaining a safe space. If one program does not meet this standard of care, another program nearby probably will, and a conscientious parent will place his or her child there.

Preschool teachers have an awesome responsibility because they have to be attentive to so much in order to keep the children safe while they are in the program space. Examining the environment for potential hazards is the first step to ensuring a safe experience. Next, teachers have to set high standards of practice for themselves and their teams, and endeavor to meet or beat those standards on a daily basis. In this chapter, we will review safety and health practices and define strategies for providing excellent care in both areas.

SAFETY CONTINGENCY PLANS

The Boys Scouts have the right idea and their motto sums it well: "Be Prepared." When working with young children, leave nothing to chance. Think through and anticipate every possible situation in advance, and define policies and procedures to address them so when something happens you have a plan. Know what the procedures are and follow them.

What situations and eventualities should be planned for as a rule? Have a clear procedure in place for the arrival and departure of the children, as well as one that defines the staffing across the day and teacher responsibilities inside and outside of the classroom. Define a stranger policy, as well as emergency contingency plans for evacuation or lockdown.

Have teachers trained and prepared for emergency care and response, and review procedures for different health issues (e.g., seizure disorders) or situations (e.g., broken teeth) that may require immediate attention. Maintain the proper teacher-child ratio, and boost adult numbers in situations where more eyes and hands may be needed.

When things run like clockwork, we smile. Everything easily falls into place; nothing gives us pause. Ideally, early childhood classrooms operate that way. Anticipate. Act. Prevent.

Accounting for the People in the Classroom

Maintain accurate attendance records and keep them in an accessible place. Know who is present and absent. Require parents to sign their children in and out each day, and have them list a phone number where they can be reached on the sheet. If any special instructions are given—for example, if a grandparent is picking up the child at lunchtime or a child is going home with a classmate for a playdate after school—have the parent note the change on the sheet so there is a written record on file. This will eliminate confusion at the end of the day because the information is in writing and not being passed along verbally.

Some preschool teachers like to spice up their daily routines by not following this simple procedure. Consider the full ramifications of this practice not being followed. What would happen if there was not an accurate attendance notebook with current contact information and then there was a fire drill or a real emergency? The margin for error in this situation is huge. Are all the children accounted for? Do we have nine or ten children today? Where can I reach Mom at 10:30 A.M.? Did they say the neighbor would pick up the child today? Did Dad mention this playdate before he left this morning?

I learned this lesson the hard way, and it left a lasting impression. I headed a team of three teachers, in a Twos class with 12 children. After a warm and active playtime on the outdoor playground, the children asked for water upon our return to the classroom. As the group came in, the solid wood, windowless door closed behind me. I asked the children to sit at the table, and went to get water. It was then that I noticed that one seat remained empty. To my horror, I was missing a little boy! A community building housed our preschool, and our classroom was situated near the pool, two locker rooms, and the central lobby.

I jumped up and ran out of the room. Fortunately, I found the little guy standing right outside the door . . . right by his irate mother. Although he was okay, she was furious but understanding; I was a complete basket case! After that, I always kept a head count as we moved about the building, went to and from the playground space, and whenever we broke into small-group activities. We kept vigilant attendance sheets by the door and always knew the "whos, whats, and wheres" from that day forward. Luck was with us that day, but the "what ifs" plagued me for a long time after— what if the boy had gone into the locker room with a "less than whole-some" stranger, or, worse, the pool area? What if he made it out the lobby doors to the parking lot? My motto became "Never again."

Efficient preschools have dropoff/pickup procedures well in hand. They follow a simple and effective plan. For instance, when parents and children enter the room in the morning, a teacher greets them at the door and asks the parent to sign the child in and note any special instructions on a pad designated for that purpose (e.g., plans for early pickup, play-dates, neighbor pickups). They store the information in the same place. Some programs ask the child to sign in as well so a double record is main-tained, and the child gets some extra writing practice. Before leaving, the teacher and parent might briefly chat.

Some preschools request either that a child be present by a specific time, such as a morning meeting, or that the parent call to say that the child will be late. That way, attendance can be taken at the same time each day; the teacher can finalize it, put the sheet in the binder, and return it to its desig-nated place by the door, so if an emergency arises, the teacher can scoop up the binder and focus on the children. Lastly, all staff members can access the information across shift changes. A simple plan like this makes emergency situations easier to manage and the daily routine less complicated.

In today's world, we must take serious precautions to keep children safe—from strangers and sometimes even family members. For example, a family was once embroiled in a nasty divorce, complete with a restrain-ing order prohibiting the father from picking up his child from preschool. One day, the father called the school, declared that he was on his way, and said no one had the right to stop him. Immediately, the mother was called as well as the police. The child was removed from the group and taken to the director's office where she sat with her teacher. Fortunately, the police met the man in the parking lot; he never made it into the build-ing. The crisis was averted. Yet, the whole situation begs the questions:

> **Point**—Establish a firm sign-in and sign-out policy with parents and maintain accurate attendance records each day. Have parents note, in writing, any third-party pickup arrangements and place notes where late-shift staff can see them. Keep the emergency contact card current for each child, and periodically verify contact telephone numbers with parents.

> **Point**—Have staff members sign in and sign out each day and keep their emergency contact information current and on hand.

What would have happened if the father had not called first? What if he came into the building? What if he met us while on the playground or on a nature walk? We can only speculate. Teachers and administrators *must* have a plan for that very possibility because bad things can and do happen. Our job—first, last, and always—must be to keep all of the children safe at every moment.

In sum, maintain good records, know who is present and absent each day, keep a head count when transitioning so it is clear that all the children are together, know who can and cannot pick up the children, and have current contact information on file and handy for when it is needed. Get to know the families and be aware of information that will make the job easier.

Lastly, have a procedure for securing building entrances and a policy regarding visitors. The following example will demonstrate why that is necessary.

A strange man unexpectedly entered a Threes classroom one morning and started looking around. He startled the teacher and the group. The teacher raced over, asked what she could do for him, and then quickly escorted him out of the room. She directed him to the main office, explaining that he could not enter the classroom area without first meeting the director. Luckily, the teacher was able to think on her feet and potentially averted a bad situation. This time, the man was harmless and nothing terrible transpired. Yet, recent history has shown that preschools are not exempt from tragedy. It is our job to keep bad things from passing through our program doors.

Lock exterior doors to safeguard the children and the staff. Initiate a "buzz-in" procedure so random people cannot enter the building. Develop a contingency plan for when the children are on the playground and an unwanted visitor arrives. Always carry a cell phone or walkie-talkie to contact someone for help.

> **Point**—Keep all exterior doors locked and establish a procedure for entry. Have a security system (a code or password system to enter the building or pick up a child) in place to protect the children and staff from unwanted visitors.

Accounting for the People on the Playground

Transitions for gross-motor play and outdoor time can breed confusion. Staff members are so focused on getting children prepared that a great deal of time elapses and children become testy. Some preschools use outdoor time as "break time" for the full-time staff and send out "floaters" with the group. Some programs split the groups so small contingents leave with a teacher as they are ready, thereby making the wait shorter. Noting these tendencies, it is easy to see how groups can fall out of ratio. The last thing we want is the teacher-child supervision to be out of balance. Child safety will definitely suffer if it does.

Once, a group of 18 three-year-olds was going outside with three teachers. Unfortunately, the communication between the teachers broke down and created a horrible situation. The first teacher led the children to the playground and held the door as the group and the two other teachers passed. Feeling the group was sufficiently covered, the head teacher returned to the room to set up activities. The second teacher escorted a child to the bathroom, believing the other two teachers could cover the action. She did not announce that she was leaving. The third teacher turned her focus to a child who fell and scraped his knee and brought him inside to get a Band-Aid. Sixteen children were on the playground with just me, the observer. Almost as if on cue, all three teachers looked out of different windows in horror, realizing what had happened. I never saw women move so fast. Hopefully, they communicated a little better from that day forward.

If the teacher-child ratio is not respected, the outcome can be hazardous. One day, a Fours class decided to split in two for morning activities—half of the group stayed inside to do a project with one teacher, and the other half went to the playground for some much-needed gross-motor time with the other teacher. Both groups were within ratio.

It was a hot summer day; the group of 10 children followed their teacher to a distant playground under some trees. Within 5 minutes, a child had a seizure and fell to the ground. The teacher did not know what she should do—focus on the nine scared children or the one in distress. She had no way to contact the building for help—no walkie-talkie, no cell phone. She

Point—Staff members should not take their breaks during the children's outdoor time because accidents are most likely to occur then. If a program has "floating" staff members, it would be beneficial to have them outdoors as much as possible to assist in supervising the children. Hopefully, these extra eyes and ears will help to prevent accidents.

knew she could not send a 4-year-old child back to the building, across a parking lot, down a set of stairs, and into the program space, which was locked to keep out intruders to get help. She could not leave the ill child unattended, nor could she calm the remaining children, who were scattering. She was in real trouble.

Fortunately, within moments of the seizure's onset, an administrator came outside to retrieve something from his car. The teacher screamed for help. He ran over, called 911, and then called the classroom on his cell phone. The director raced out and assisted the child having the seizure, and the teacher turned to the rest of the group and tried to calm them and bring them back inside. When the ambulance came, the director went with the child, and the administrator called the parents to meet them at the hospital. Once inside, both teachers had a group meeting to help the children understand what happened and calm their fears. That day, I witnessed the best and the worst planning, as well as some divine intervention.

Fortunately, everything turned out all right. The child had only a febrile seizure, so he was treated and released that day. The administrators smoothly transferred the child to appropriate care. The teachers honestly answered a lot of questions asked by the group. Yet, that momentary lapse in coverage could have ended much worse. For instance, a child could have wandered off while the teacher attended to the ailing child. The group could have become hysterical and hard to calm or control, and/or the teacher could have reacted poorly under the stress and frozen.

The point needs to be stressed—a program should always have adequate staffing or procedures in place for such a situation. Sometimes luck is not on our side and an extra person is not standing nearby.

Be prepared! While outdoors, carry a cell phone or a walkie-talkie, just in case, and always bring emergency contact information and a medical kit when children leave the classroom. Train all staff members in CPR and first aid and periodically receive training for immediate care emergencies (e.g., sudden-onset seizure, a badly bleeding cut, or broken bone) and review them often, especially with new staff members. Most important, increase staffing when children leave the safety of the classroom. Be proactive. Never take anything for granted.

While outdoors on the playground, assign stations for each teacher so all children can be easily supervised. Make sure areas obscured from direct view are covered by the teachers. If possible, have one teacher supervise riding toys on the hard surface; have another by the swings, slides, and climbing equipment; and another supervising children in game play, ball play, or those engaged in small-group discovery, such as finding worms. Add an additional person to the ratio to accompany a child or small group inside for toileting, water, or first aid.

Point—Before transitioning to the outdoor playground, have the children use the toilet so return trips are minimized. Carry water with you outdoors as well as tissues and a first aid kit so supplies are on hand.

Teachers should refrain from engaging in personal conversations while outside and instead focus on the children. No longer confined or restrained by furnishings or walls, they like to move as quickly as they can! Be prepared, for this is the land of running feet and outdoor voices. Provide vigilant oversight. Raise the level of supervision and have more eyes on the group, because children require extra guidance when engaged in active outdoor play.

Now let's focus on healthy classroom/teacher practice.

CREATING A HEALTHY PRESCHOOL EXPERIENCE

Early childhood programs must do everything in their power to provide a healthy environment for the children. Teachers and administrators must define policies for standards of health and good practices to optimize healthy living.

Preschool Health Policies

Delineate the preschool's policies and procedures in the parent and staff handbooks so everyone is aware of them in advance of entry or hiring. This will help ensure a healthy environment for all. Clearly state in the parent handbook that all children must complete an annual physical, receive all vaccinations, and have parents submit signed documentation indicating such, which will be kept on file at the school. Delineate policies and procedures for denying ill children entry to school and provide a list of conditions or illnesses that will prevent children from attending, such as fever, diarrhea, vomiting, rash, and pinkeye. Outline mandatory time frames for contagious illness and define the policy allowing for a child's return, such as a doctor's note. Describe the process for caring for children who become ill while at school, the call-home procedures, and the expectations for parent response in this event. Indicate whether or not medication will be administered onsite and, if so, by whom (e.g., teacher, director, nurse) and explain how medication will be handled and stored. Include policies on the administration of topical sunscreen as well.

If the preschool requires all children to be fully toilet-trained, define the expectations for parental assistance if a child has more than one accident and policies for recourse or even removal. If the program has a more liberal standard for toilet-training, define the policies around diapering and toileting, and list the required items (e.g., diapers, pull-ups, wipes, creams) that must be provided and resupplied by the parents.

If there are health concerns, such as children who have peanut allergies, create and publish a policy to address it, such as designating the preschool as a nut-free zone. Be proactive and clear about the expectations of the program.

Preparing for Allergies

Many young children have allergies (e.g., food, animal, chemical); note and respect them. Before a child enrolls, ask parents for allergy information so the proper precautions can be put in place to keep the child safe.

Many preschools, in their effort to protect children from anaphylactic shock or death, have adopted stringent food rules. There are many nut-free schools throughout the country as a result. Some programs limit acceptable foods to a specific list that parents and guardians can bring to the classroom; others remove all outside sources and provide all the food themselves. Most programs allow children to bring their own snacks and meals into the classroom from home. To maintain health and safety, allergies should be posted so everyone is aware.

Some teachers believe that privacy should be respected, so personal information should not be in plain view. Others feel it should be clearly marked. Why not adopt a solution that satisfies both groups and protects the health, welfare, and privacy of the children? Make a chart with the word *ALLERGIES* boldly written across the top of the page. List all allergies and/or health issues that require immediate action, place a picture of the child near his or her name for fast reference and to reduce error, and denote the specific allergy, the location of the medication if onsite, and

Point—Clearly mark the location of medication for children in the room. Medication should be kept in locked boxes that can be quickly accessed. Have the key or combination nearby for quick retrieval. Also mark the location of the first aid kit, by placing a red cross above it. Lastly, have individual containers of topical sunscreen for each child and use a new pair of gloves when applying it to each child. A telephone should be available in each classroom so that an emergency call can be made without delay.

the protocol for its treatment. Hang this chart in a prominent place in the room, such as on the refrigerator. To protect privacy, place a blank page over the personal information but leave the header, *ALLERGIES*, visible. Now, everyone knows allergy information is posted, but only those who need to access it will do so. Of course, teachers should commit allergy information to memory. But if a problem arises while a substitute or other temporary caregiver is in the room, the information is available.

Simple Hygiene Practices Offset the Spread of Illness

Health-related routines done in the classroom require extra scrutiny, especially food preparation, hygiene, naptime practices, and toileting. Although it is possible to take this to extremes, it is better to be overcautious than lax.

Every year countless children die from illnesses and contagious diseases contracted from the environment. Some are spread through the air (e.g., influenza, tuberculosis), some through direct personal contact (e.g., hepatitis or rotavirus), through foods (e.g., *E. coli*, salmonella), or through contact with animals or reptiles (e.g., *E. coli*, salmonella).

Although we cannot protect children from every disease that exists, we can minimize their contact through some simple and effective hygienic practices—the most obvious being proactive hand washing.

People consistently challenge my views on the subject. Many assert that coming into contact with germs makes a body's defenses stronger. That is true, to a point. Children will find germs in the course of a regular day's play, so it seems short-sighted not to teach and encourage hand washing, which could potentially offset a horrible health experience. As teachers, we can influence young children early so they learn to be safe and clean. Hopefully, lasting habits will form that promote good hygiene.

Hand Washing—The First Defense Against Illness

Kids will be kids. They go on nose-mining expeditions, suck their thumbs, drool, wipe runny noses on the backs of their hands or sleeves, miss when they use the toilet, and/or have trouble cleaning themselves in the bathroom. As a result, they need to clean their hands throughout the day to prevent the spread of illness. Since they touch everything, including their teachers, they should learn to keep their hands clean. As a matter of practice, we should, too.

Considering the number of surfaces children touch in a given day, it is prudent to teach them to how to wash their hands effectively. Teachers must teach children proper hand-washing procedures to ensure that enough soap, water, time, and effort are used. They should also monitor the children as they wash their hands to ensure compliance. Teachers must be role models, washing their own hands throughout the day to make it a standard process in the environment.

Some teachers have children sing a song, such as "Twinkle, Twinkle Little Star," while they wash so they spend enough time at the sink. Others spritz the liquid soap into their hands to make sure it is used. At minimum, children should spend 10 seconds vigorously washing all hand surfaces with liquid soap and warm water before drying their hands with a paper towel.

When considering the daily routine, key points for hand washing can be identified for both the children and the adults: upon arrival to the classrooms; before and after eating or preparing food; after toileting; after touching animals; before and after contact with sand, water, or play dough; and upon return from gross-motor activity (indoor or outdoor). Let's consider each of these scenarios in depth.

Washing Hands upon Each Entry to the Classroom

Since we don't know what children do in the backseat of the car, they should clean their hands upon entering the classroom. In fact, teachers should teach by example and demonstrate the correct procedure for hand washing throughout the day. Make a point of cleaning your hands when you walk into the room, after visiting the adult or children's bathroom, and upon returning from outdoor play or any gross-motor activity. If the children see you habitually do this, it will seem less foreign and they will more likely to do it as well.

Children will be children. They don't willingly wash their hands, so be insistent. After all, this may be the only place where they learn good hygiene. Assume that it is and be dedicated to that end. Don't ask if they washed, because many claim they did. Instead, watch for the errant child who tries to avoid the task. Lastly, pay attention when children toss out the paper towel. Often, children wash well, then cancel it out by lifting the trash can lid with their clean hand to toss away a paper towel. If there is a lidded trash can, remove it so no one touches it.

> **Point**—Adults and children should frequently wash their hands during the day (e.g., upon entry in the classroom; before and after playing with play dough, sand, or water; upon return from gross-motor activity; before and after eating; and after toileting).

Washing Hands Before and After Eating

Without question, children should be required to wash their hands before eating. It makes absolute sense. We want them ingesting only the food that is served and nothing else.

One summer, something very sad and frightening happened to a child from my Twos class. The family purchased prepackaged, prewashed vegetables that were contaminated with remnants of manure and/or a manure-based fertilizer at the store. A wonderful, vibrant little boy became violently ill from ingesting *E. coli* bacteria: His kidneys failed, he was in and out of consciousness for weeks, and he was hospitalized for months. Unfortunately, pressure from accumulating fluid in the skull caused visual impairment. The little child lost years of his life relearning and reacquiring what he had already known—all because the vegetables he ate were not truly "ready to eat."

After learning that, we made sure to wash everything before serving or eating it and became much more cautious while handling food, preparing for meals, and especially washing hands. Some fellow teachers chose to be less stringent about cleaning, washing hands, and preparing food. Still others were completely complacent, applying the "3-second rule" when food or utensils hit the floor. Best practice dictates that teachers are dedicated to providing a clean and healthy snack/meal experience for the children. Although it might take time to wash hands twice, three times, or more, it will always be worth the effort. A little child's life, or quality of life, might depend on it.

Once children wash hands for a snack or a meal, have them sit at the cleaned table. I have often seen children wash their hands and then go sit on the rug for story while lunch is set up (a highly counterproductive practice, since they must rewash after touching the floor or carpet while seated there). If the food requires time for preparation, delay washing or seat the children at the table, and sing a song or read a story to them while they wait.

Washing Hands After Toileting

Remember that children can become seriously ill by coming into contact with fecal contamination on surfaces or by touching animals. Let's first consider people as a source of contamination. Not washing hands thoroughly and completely after toileting can be a source of illness. "Residue" left on a child's hands after wiping his bottom can easily be left anywhere he touches if his hands are not properly cleaned. Young children need guidance and supervision when washing hands. If an adult is not

> **Point**—Clean and sanitize the bathroom sinks using a bleach solution or multiple bleach wipes on the basin, knobs, and faucet to ensure that no cross-contamination occurs. Periodically clean the bathroom doorknobs or handles and the flusher on the toilet bowl as well.

present, a child's unclean hands can touch the faucet, knobs, or sink basin, thereby placing every other child who follows at risk for *E. coli*.

Furthermore, best practice dictates that one sink be used for toileting and a different one for food prep; such separation reduces the chance of cross-contamination. However, if two sinks are out of the question, and only a bathroom sink is available for hand washing, the teacher should thoroughly clean and sanitize the sink basin, faucet, and knobs using a bleach solution after the last child uses the toilet and washes his or her hands there. In addition, all counter surfaces that children touch should be cleaned. This should routinely be done before any subsequent child uses that sink for hand washing in advance of eating snack or a meal. Many ask, "Who has time to do this?" The answer is: A teacher does, and must.

Washing Hands After Touching Animals

Many preschool classrooms have pets. Before bringing a pet into the room, teachers should make sure there are no children with allergies to fur or dander. If there are no allergies, adding a bunny, guinea pig, or gerbil can be a good way to teach responsibility and respect. The children can learn to feed and water the animals, keep them safe and healthy, and treat them humanely.

Children should be vigilant about hand washing after touching the animal or the cage. Small animals do not watch where they step or what they roll around in when they are in their habitats. As a result, the children could be exposed to "remnants" when they touch their beloved pets.

> **Point**—If children handle the classroom pet, make sure they thoroughly wash their hands with soap and warm water afterward. Keep the pet cage clean, change the flooring materials frequently, and place cages in areas that are easy to maintain. Have cages over uncarpeted floors so messes can be swept or mopped up easily.

Some preschools offer in-house field trips, where aquariums bring marine life to the classroom, or go offsite to visit a local farm or petting zoo, and undoubtedly, the children come in contact with animals. Be sure to apply the same level of care and follow hygiene rules after these excursions so children stay healthy. Wash their hands with soap and water as soon as possible, and in the interim use hand sanitizer.

Some programs have melodic caged birds that tweet and chirp throughout the day. Be vigilant about keeping the area clean; otherwise, the area can become soiled with molted feathers, discarded shells, and seed.

Reconsider some classroom pets, such as turtles, altogether, because salmonella can be contracted by handling reptiles and snakes. If the classroom already has a turtle, keep it in its enclosure.

Hermit crabs have become the new "shelled creature" of choice in many preschool classrooms because they are so easy to maintain. Many crawl around with brightly painted shells and hold a place of honor in the science area. As with any pet, keep them healthy, well watered, and well fed, and make sure that children couple "pet contact" with hand washing *every* time. The same should be true of frogs or toads.

Some programs have fish tanks that hold a beta fish or some goldfish. Little children love to feed the fish and watch them ravenously attack the morsels that float on the water. Be sure that children wash and thoroughly rinse their hands before feeding them so as not make the fish sick from soap residue. Have the children wash their hands so they don't ingest the fish food.

Washing Hands Before and After Sand, Water, or Play Dough

For health's sake, children should wash their hands before and after touching the sand and water at the sensory table and the play dough. Without fail, young children sneeze and cough all over the contents of the sensory table and all over the play dough. As a matter of practice, teachers should wash at these times as well.

Play dough can be contaminated with even more germs, so be sure to change it frequently. As a group, make new dough as a science and math activity, and have the children measure the ingredients and mix them together. By replacing it often, we reduce the spread of illness.

Once during a program visit, a child invited me to play with some dough. I took up a piece and started molding it. I asked the teacher if she had recently added sand for texture. She said no. Within a second, I recalled how many children I saw exploring their noses that day and immediately dropped it. Now I knew what was in the dough. Yuck. I had to go wash my hands.

Teach Good Hygiene—Sneezing and/or Coughing

Children do not engage in the most health-conscious practice as a rule. They suck their thumbs and then touch the classroom materials; they pick their noses and then read a book. They put their hands down their pants and then give hugs. When these practices occur, teachers need to be proactive and have the children wash their hands.

Many children openly cough and sneeze all over toys, puzzles, books, the food on the table, and even the teacher.

Coughing and sneezing openly spreads illness. Think of how quickly the common cold moves from one person to the next. Adults and children should learn to effectively contain their coughs and sneezes to prevent the spread of germs.

Teachers should show children how to cough and sneeze into their elbows, not into their hands. If children do sneeze or cough into their hand, remind them to wash right away. This prevents the spread of germs through hand contact or transfer.

Some teachers are poor role models. They openly sneeze, cough, and/or blow their noses without washing afterward. Some put used tissues in their pocket or stuff them up their sleeve. If the adults don't follow the correct procedure, why should the children? Show children how to use a tissue, how to toss it out, and then have them wash their hands.

To maintain a healthy preschool environment, always remember to clean the toys when they are soiled or have been placed in a child's mouth. Young children forget that during pretend play, they should not place toys and classroom materials in their mouths. Since they still require guidance as they adapt to preschool, help them remember not to put toys, such as pretend foods, play utensils, and other objects, into their mouths. Whenever they do so, be sure to take the item, remove it to the sink, and thoroughly clean it with a bleach solution before returning it to the center. Wipe the item dry and make certain that no bleach water is trapped within it that might later leak out.

Each teacher plays a key role in creating a healthy environment. It should not be a job left to the head teachers, an assistant teacher, or an aide. Each and every adult should show a child how to act, what to do, and how to behave—by example.

Point—Have boxes of tissues scattered throughout the room for easy access.

Point—If possible, place plastic toys in a dishwasher to clean and sanitize them.

6

Best Teacher Practice— Establishing Sound Daily Care Routines

The daily care routines of preschool are numerous, and they encompass a large part of the time a child is present in the classroom. Teachers have to use this time well to create meaningful experiences.

Personal care routines are conducted individually, in small-group settings, and with the large group overall. They include points of basic care, such as meal and snack time, nap or rest time, and time spent toileting and washing up.

PREPARING FOR HEALTHY SNACK AND MEAL TIME

When children eat in the preschool classroom, every precaution must be taken to provide a sanitary setting and fresh, nutritious, unspoiled foods. Employ high standards when preparing and presenting food to the children. Use the proper utensils and make sure gloves are used when handling food. If children help with the mealtime routine, monitor what they do to ensure hygiene.

A few procedures must be carried out with care before food is introduced. First, clean all surfaces, such as counters where food is prepared and tables on which it is served. Use a spray bleach solution and paper towels to clean the spaces. Do not use sponges because they are loaded with germs, mold, and mildew. When cleaning the tables, spray the bleach solution only when children are not present. Let it sit for a few seconds to sanitize the space. Use the towel to completely clean the tabletop and the edges of the table. Wipe off any remaining residue.

When handling food, wear gloves and use clean utensils. If meals are provided by the center, keep the food covered with plastic until it is offered. If children bring in their own snacks and meals, use gloves when handing the food and opening the packages. Never open packaging with scissors from the art cart or by using teeth. If food drops to the floor, discard it immediately and provide more food to the hungry child. Remind the children not to eat food from the floor, or they likely will.

Snack as a Center Choice

In some programs, rather than requiring everyone to sit for a snack at the same time, children can choose to have snack as a free-choice activity. This is good developmental practice and it allows children to assess whether they want to eat or not. Many children take advantage of it and enjoy a quick bite and drink between play areas. However, just like other centers in the room, the snack table needs to be monitored.

The snack table must be sanitized with each new child who sits for snack, so a teacher should be nearby to clean it. If a child coughs on the table while having snack or picks at his nose and the space is not cleaned, the next child seated there will be ingesting more than graham crackers. Without hesitation, the table should be *safely* cleaned—that is, no child should be seated at the table when the cleaning solution is sprayed. Never spray a hazardous chemical while someone is seated in the area. As small people, children get direct exposure to the fumes.

Some programs believe that by using place mats for each meal they can bypass the table cleaning process. Place mats may make it easier for children to know where they sit, but they need to be cleaned and sanitized before and after eating, just like the table.

Put out only enough food for one or two children at a time. Be attentive to the food once it is put out. Keep it covered to prevent spoilage. Put out only enough cups, napkins, plates, and utensils as needed; otherwise, some will likely fall to the floor and need to be tossed out. The next child should not eat his or her snack with dirty utensils or unclean paper products.

Remind the children to take what they touch and eat what they take. Have them discard what they do not eat. Pay attention here. Sometimes children put food or drink back in the basket, bowl, or pitcher. If this hap-

> **Point**—When cleaning the snack area, spray the bleach, let it sit a minute, and then thoroughly clean it with a damp cloth. Eating off a bleach-covered surface can be dangerous—get off as much residue as you can. Wipe the table edges as well as the top surface when bleaching the tables. Clean the chair surfaces periodically. Do not use sponges; they carry germs. Use paper towels.

pens, toss it out and get fresh food or drink. Be nearby while the children snack, so problems can be prevented. It just takes a little extra effort.

Snack as a Whole-Group Routine

Some programs have meal time as a group. It is easier in this context for teachers to monitor the process and engage in conversation with the children. Some programs move to a cafeteria space and refrain from eating in the classroom; others sit at the classroom tables and share a meal. Some programs provide snack foods and meals; others have the food sent in each day with the child.

If children bring in their own food, it should be stored in a refrigerator so milk and prepared food don't spoil. Some programs have the children store their lunchboxes in their cubbies. Either way, when the lunchboxes are brought to the table, refrain from having them placed on the clean table surfaces. Lunchboxes are often treated as simple devices for toting items. They are often placed on the floor in the car or classroom. They are likely to be germ breeding grounds where spilled milk, leaky containers, and overripe foods were once stored. Placing these soiled boxes on clean table surfaces negates the process of cleaning.

It is good to involve children in daily routines. Many like to help, especially if their job for the day is setting the table. Have table helpers wash their hands and stay focused on the job. Monitor them as they do the work and watch for errant practices (e.g., nose mining; brushing their hands against their mouth, nose, or hair), and remind them to rewash their hands if they engage in any nonhygienic practices.

When passing out utensils, give children spoons and forks in easy-to-hold cups, with the handles up, so children do not touch the spoon bowls or fork tines. Have them hold the outside of the cups rather than putting their hand inside them. This will help prevent the cups from falling. If the cups do fall, throw them away and make sure they are not put on the table. Hand children a small number of napkins rather than a big pile. Give them only as many as they need. When they have too much to hold, children drop things. If teachers assist in picking up the fallen items, both adult and child must rewash their hands before proceeding with the task.

Point—When using gloves at meal time, have a pair of scissors (designated solely for food use) near the table. It makes opening packages much easier. Discourage children from opening their food wrappers with their teeth.

CREATING A REASSURING NAP AND REST TIME

Naptime! Many teachers look forward to this break in the day and often use it to recoup and regroup themselves. Naptime allows everyone to prepare for the rest of the day or the rest of the week if it is used as prep time. Yet, despite it being "down" time, naptime still requires attention and should employ good health practices.

Cleanliness Is Next to Sleepiness

Let's first look at cleanliness. Are the cots used only for specific children? Are the cots soiled? How clean are the children's personal items (e.g., the linens children sleep on and sleep with)? How clean is the general space used for nap and rest?

Providing Sleep Surfaces: Cots

If a program offers a period in the day for napping or resting, suitable furnishings need to be provided. Some preschools provide mats for rest time, and should rethink this practice. Fabric mats can become soiled and can hold onto germs, since the surface is permeable. Since children have "accidents" in their sleep, the foam- or fiber-filled pad can become damaged. Vinyl mats are no better if they have cracks or tears in the covering. Plus, vinyl mats do not allow for airflow and reflect the child's body heat, often making them sweat as they sleep. When children perspire, drool, or have "accidents," liquid can be absorbed by the foam and become a breeding ground for germs. It would be best to upgrade from vinyl or fabric floor mats to raised plastic canvas mesh cots. The reason is simple: Cots can be cleaned and sanitized easily and there is less chance that the cots will become soiled and need to be removed.

Thus, most preschools offer small child-sized cots for the children to rest on. Typically, the cots are solid and firm, are raised off the floor, and have mesh netting so there is air exchange. Since the cots are made of plastic, the surface should be covered with a fitted sheet so the child is not resting directly on it. Periodically, teachers must clean and sanitize the cots, because nothing smells more nauseating than old drool or excrement on the plastic mesh cots.

Each child should be assigned his or her own cot. Since illness can easily be transferred on surfaces, and since children may "christen" their cot in some way during sleep, cots should not be interchanged. Furthermore, each child should have a designated nap spot in the classroom so he or she can acclimate before falling asleep.

Some programs absorb the expense of the nap sheets so parents do not have to provide cot covers. Some even provide small blankets to the children that are laundered onsite to ensure cleanliness. Others provide blankets and cot sheets so every child can be adequately covered and comfortable during rest. These items are usually laundered at home.

Personal Nap Items

Most programs ask families to provide the linens needed for a comfy nap time. If so, be specific so parents understand what should be provided and how it will maintained.

Nap items may consist of a cot cover (e.g., crib-sized sheet or beach towel), a blanket, and a small pillow. In addition, a cozy stuffed animal or security blanket may be provided. Preschool teachers should clearly ask parents to supply child-sized items so king-sized comforters and full-size pillows will not be sent. Show the parents the size of the storage space for nap items and ask them to provide items that will easily fit inside it.

Define the expectations for the care and cleaning of these items. If parents are responsible for laundering the linens, make that clear and provide the rationale behind the practice. Tell the parents that unclean linens can put a child at risk for illness and/or lice. Fresh and clean nap items make children feel valued and help them get cozy. Dirty and smelly linens do the opposite. Thus, pack up the nap items on Friday and send them home with a note thanking the parents for cleaning them. Get them in the habit of washing the items or replacing them with suitable alternates. Kind and gentle reminders might be necessary on occasion when the items are returned in the same shape as when they left.

A Clean Space to Rest

On a regular basis, clean the floor and vacuum the carpets where children sleep. Check the area for small items that were dropped during the day and could pose a choking hazard to curious children. Remove temptations, such as toys and books, and encourage sleep versus play. Remove shoes and place them away from the nap space to prevent engaging exploration. Children depend on a teacher's vigilance in providing a safe and clean space.

A case in point: One day while observing a program, I noticed a bug on the floor. It looked like a little ant, except it had wings. I stood up and stepped on it, then cleaned up the spot with a tissue. A few minutes later, I saw two more bugs and repeated the process. Within an hour, I saw nearly 30 more bugs coming up from the cracks in the floor tiles. Then I realized what they were: termites, winged and ready to swarm after the recent hot weather and cooling rain.

I told the teacher, who acknowledged the problem and said they had scheduled an exterminator to come the next week. So, for the next few days, the children would be sleeping close to the floor where an infestation was brewing. Maybe they were not in direct contact with the bugs yet, but their little blankets draped down to the floor.

Unfortunately, I left the center before naptime, so I do not know what actually happened that day or any other day that week. I wondered how the room would be treated (with chemicals, organic pesticides?) and if it would be clean and safe after the treatment. After all, the children play on and rest close to the floor. The only thing that was left for me to do was hope it would be done soon and done well.

Be Extra Kind: The Most Vulnerable Point in a Child's Day

One last thing: Be kind to the children as they fall asleep. They are vulnerable at this time of the day. Often, they push through their exhaustion or actively fight sleep in order not to miss anything. Many children become overtired, and this can tax their patience and physical systems. Remember, it is hard work being a preschooler. In the course of the day, children are mastering new concepts and skills, making and keeping friends, and endeavoring to successfully control their bodily functions. Thus, young children need rest, and they require calm, nonagitated sleep.

The perceptive teacher knows that taking an extra second or two to pat children's backs or tousle their hair will help settle them. Teachers know it is best to sit close by a child for a while to provide that extra sense of comfort and safety. Some will even read a short, simple story to help lull children's tired minds into a state of rest. Treat the young children in your care with love and kindness. They are only small for a short time.

Best Practice: Naptime

Teachers cannot prevent termite infestations, but they can prevent the spread of lice and/or illness. Routinely store each child's nap items (e.g., small blanket, cot sheet, and pillow) in his or her own sealable plastic container. This keeps the items compact, clean, and contained so they do not hang out of the cubby and touch other children's personal items or fall on the floor and get stepped on by little feet. Less than optimal preschool programs follow a less hygienic practice and store nap items between the stacked cots, enabling the transfer of lice and illness (e.g., rotavirus), or stuff them into the cubbies where they can hang out or fall.

No preschool wants to spread disease, for once a virus enters the space, it can wreak havoc on a program and stay in the classroom for long stretches. For instance, we know that once one child gets a tummyache and diarrhea, everyone becomes sick. The virus moves with alacrity from one person to another. Although insufficient hand washing might be one cause, unhealthy naptime practices may also play a role. Therefore, assign cots to individual children by name or number for the school year, keep the nap items in sealable bins, and periodically clean the cots with a bleach solution.

Next, consider the amount of space that exists between children at naptime. Ideally, cots should be spaced so little to no physical contact occurs between children. The optimal distance around each cot should be a 36-inch bubble. In closer spaces, separate cots by a solid barrier. Why? Not all children sleep during naptime. Many roll around and engage in "personal discovery" activities. Therefore, when they reach over and touch one another, they could be sharing quite a bit. Remind children to keep their fingers out of their noses and pant belts, and when they do, have them wash.

Encourage self-help skills by asking the children to set up their cots. Have them carry their nap items to their cot and encourage partners to help set up their cots together. Remove any bags or boxes that stored the nap items for safety's sake.

Dim the lights, draw the curtains, and put on soft music, then watch children drop off one by one into blissful, snore-filled slumber.

OPTIMIZING THE TOILETING ROUTINE

The last personal care routine that requires attention is diapering and toileting. When this is done well, the child feels proud of him- or herself; when it is done poorly, a child feels shameful and resistant, which can lead to increased accidents and many unhappy moments.

Since some children are in the process of becoming potty-trained, let's first discuss diapering. There have been times when I wasn't sure if I was in a daycare center or a rodeo. I have seen little children hoisted to the table and extracted from their clothes in a matter of microseconds. Skillfully and nimbly, the adult holds the child's little legs between two adult fingers while the other hand quickly disengages the tapes and removes the diaper in one fell swoop. In what seems like a flash, the next diaper is slid under the bare bottom and the legs are released, leaving the adult only to fasten the tapes and slide the child back into his or her clothes. It seems very similar to the process of roping a calf—lasso it, knock it onto its back, tie its legs together, then rise and take a bow.

Obviously, this approach may have clear and understandable repercussions. No wonder children are resistant and run around the room, screaming "No!" Who would want to be treated that way?

Respect the child when diapering and be socially proactive. Use the process as a learning opportunity and as a chance for social bonding. While removing the diaper, talk about the process. Ask her to hold the diaper. Comment on the sound of the tape as it pulls off, or talk about cool air she feels when the diaper is removed. Ask her to sing a song as the diaper is maneuvered and have her help replace her clothes. It does not take much to change a moment from bad to good. After all, this is a vulnerable moment for a child, so be kind and respectful.

Toileting requires a different strategy. Rather than distracting the child as is done during diapering, the goal in toileting and/or potty-training is to assist the child in mastering a new self-help process.

The first hurdle to jump is helping the child know when he has to go to the bathroom. Since this is a relatively new experience for children, teachers must remind them until they can make that determination themselves, which comes with time and attention. Once a child feels the urge to "use the potty," then he needs supervision, assistance, and a clear path to the bathroom. Teachers should instill the belief that the child can "do it himself," but also be nearby to help children with their belt buckles and buttons.

Teachers should also be nearby for safety's sake. Once, when left alone, a child slipped while sitting on an adult-sized commode and nearly fell in. When the teacher peeked in, she discovered the little girl hanging on with her elbows, her little bottom hanging deep in the bowl. Needless to say, this was traumatizing for the child. Therefore, a teacher should be on hand, just in case something like this happens.

Always know when children leave the room to use the bathroom, and know what they are doing while there. I have seen teachers send children to the bathroom and then completely forget about them for long stretches of time.

Once, a child sneaked into the bathroom and had a wonderful time playing in the sink with the water and liquid soap. For over 12 minutes, he had a great time splashing the water and getting everything wet. By the time he was discovered, the floor was completely covered with water, the soap bottle was nearly empty, and he was soaked to the skin. Harmless fun, it would seem—unless he slipped, hit his head and fell to the floor unconscious, or became violently ill after ingesting liquid soap.

Another time, a little boy was left alone in the bathroom for nearly 7 minutes. No one checked on him. If the bathroom was just a space that contained a sink and a toilet, it might not be a problem, but this bathroom served as a storage room as well. In addition to the sink and toilet, the

> **Point**—Bathrooms should be cleaned regularly. Toilets should be checked frequently throughout the day and flushed when needed.

room contained the TV/VCR cart, an assortment of outdoor toys (e.g., jump ropes and hula hoops), a stack of puzzles on the windowsill, and an assortment of spray bottles and cleaning solutions, fortunately out of reach. It was irresponsible to leave a child alone in this space.

This begs the question—what should be stored in the bathroom? Some programs keep mops, brooms, toilet brushes, and even plungers in the bathroom or stalls. This practice should be rethought. Consider the plunger—a source of an inconceivable number of germs. To an adult, it is a gross necessity, used for the occasional "backup." But to an inquisitive child it is a new thing to explore, to touch, to sense, and an intriguing toy to play with. If the building's plumbing requires a plunger, then invest in a cabinet where it can be stored along with the toilet brush, thereby making them inaccessible. In fact, get a cabinet big enough to store the mop and broom as well.

Finally, keep an eye on the soap bottle, especially if it has the type of fun pump top that young children like to push. Always have it available, but monitor its use. I have seen many children go to use the toilet, come out of the stall, look for soap and not find it, and then either just wash with water or skip the process entirely. They need soap, so provide it.

Refrain from watering down the liquid soap. It might make it last longer, but watered-down soap is less effective. Make sure there are ample paper towels and toilet paper in the bathroom area.

In sum, young children have very limited life experience, so they need support and guidance in almost everything they do until they get the various systems in hand. Leaving them to their own devices is not the most prudent course of action. Helping them learn good practice and make good choices is the true role of an adult in a small child's life.

PREPARING FOR GROSS-MOTOR PLAYTIME

One final area requiring child-specific care is preparation for outdoor recreation. Here, teachers need to be proactive and make sure that each child is ready for outdoor play. A quick checklist should be followed before transitioning the group.

First, attend to toileting before leaving the room and, at minimum, ask if anyone needs to use the toilet. Accompanying children to the toilet to try is even better practice. This will reduce the need to return in dribs and drabs over the next 30 minutes.

Next, have the children readied for the outdoors by either dressing them for the cooler weather in appropriate attire, such as sweater and long sleeves and pants for cool days or coats, snow pants, boots, and various accessories (e.g., hats, scarves, and mittens) on cold or snowy days. In warm weather, if school policy allows the use of topical sunscreen, use a fresh glove as you apply it to each child.

On warm days, bring water outside with the group and have cups on hand for drinking. Always carry a box of tissues, a trash bag, and the first aid kit out as well. Have hand sanitizer available for gooey noses and dirty hands. When coming into contact with dirty noses or bloody scratches, use latex gloves and then discard them.

If the children ride on tricycles or big wheels, have them wear helmets to protect against head injury. It is best if each family provides a helmet for their own child, but if the school provides them, clean and sanitize them regularly.

Before bringing the children outdoors, send a "scout" ahead to clean and check the space. Look for broken glass and sharp objects.

Check the equipment for problems, such as cracks that might pinch, splintered wood that can puncture skin, or rust that can be abrasive. Close off these specific areas of potential injury from use, and report them to the administration for repair when you return to the classroom. Make sure all portable equipment (e.g., jump ropes, balls, hoops, pails, and shovels) is in good shape.

When recess is over, cover the sandbox with a weighted tarp to keep water out and animals from using it as a toilet. Return all equipment to its proper place and lock the storage unit to prevent loss or theft. Also, keep the shed locked to prevent outsiders from using it for their own purposes.

Once in the classroom, have all children wash their hands well. Remember that pressure-treated lumber is treated with arsenic, so it is toxic and hands should be washed off after touching it. Rusted metal is also dangerous and should be cleaned off skin surfaces.

In conclusion, the job of the preschool teacher is to provide a safe and healthy environment for the children who are there. We must conscientiously attend to the care of young children because they are incapable of providing preventative care for themselves. We should strive to teach them good hygiene and safety practice, but be on hand to provide it for them as long as required.

7

Enhancing Teaching Practice Through Effective Classroom Routines

In addition to the routines for personal care, other daily routines shape the learning and socialization experiences of young children. These include time set aside for large-group meetings, small-group activities, clean-up, and outdoor recreation or indoor gross-motor play. In a well-run preschool classroom, the routines are outlined on a predictable daily schedule, and children are comfortable and familiar with them.

DEFINING THE PRIME DAILY SCHEDULE

When defining a daily classroom schedule, keep in mind the needs of the children during the school day, and the methods for encouraging the learning, exploration, and discovery processes at the forefront. Make it easy to follow, and remember that the children are new to the preschool experience. Make it flow, so children can anticipate what is coming next. Make it firm, so it does not change and create confusion. Make it fun, so they want to move from point to point without difficulty.

Children are creatures of routine and of habit. Initially, they depend on adults to move them through their day and explain what is happening as they go. At the onset, they are highly dependent on others, but with time and experience, they are able to grasp what is happening and understand the nature of the routine. Before long, they are able to see how routines are done and how the day fits together. Preschoolers create contexts all the time. They define scripts or sequences for events to help make sense of them. If you ask a child what happens when they go to school, they likely will respond with some version of the following passage:

We get to play for a long time every morning, then we have morning meeting. After meeting, we get ready for snack and we have to wash our hands. Then, we go outside and play. Later we come in and do things with our teachers and our friends. Then we get ready to go home and we have to make sure Mom gets our stuff out of the cubbies.

This type of understanding is more evident as the school year progresses and children grow accustomed to the daily schedule.

The daily schedule is an integral part of the preschool experience. Young children are able to work best when they know what is coming next. They need structure and a framework within which to function. Providing a clear, predictable schedule gives them a context.

The same is true of the school day. Having a daily schedule puts the day into an ordered state. To implement an effective early learning program, consider the time frames for activities. Children need time to plan out and engage in play activities, and they need time to move from activity to activity. Clearly indicate the areas that are open and/or closed for free-choice activities. Consider the daily schedule a skeleton on which the meat of teaching and learning can be applied.

Create a plan that alternates between free play and structured activity, between large-group and smaller-group times, between teacher-directed and child-initiated learning, and between active play and quiet time. During free-choice time, allow children to choose activities and play opportunities that are personally meaningful. Furthermore, encourage children to move around to different centers, play with different children, and move freely between various groups of children. These are just part of the normal developmental routine young children need to thrive. Figure 7.1 delineates prime examples of daily schedule for preschool classrooms.

TIMING IS EVERYTHING DURING EARLY CHILDHOOD

"Timing" means allowing enough time for play and learning, so don't rush experiences. Learning comes as a process unfolds. Give the children ample time to explore and discover new ideas. Since they follow their own

> **Point**—Put the daily schedule in picture form so the children can see the activities and know what to expect without reading. Display it in a few prominent places in the classroom so adults and children can easily refer to it.

internal maturational clock, they learn new concepts and master new skills as they are developmentally ready. Be aware of developmental norms, pay attention to each child, and offer timely opportunities.

Children need ample time to choose an activity, to start play or learning, to reach a point of immersion, and then to come out of it without feeling rushed or cheated. It is a process. Thus, schedule plenty of time (at least 45 minutes, optimally an hour) for children to play, and offer *many* blocks of free-choice time throughout the day. Devote at least one-third of the program day (e.g., 3 hours for a 9-hour program) to free play. During this time, all centers should be open. When centers are closed and materials are unavailable, then learning is limited. This applies to everything in the room. Provide children ample time to work with any and all materials they wish to use.

Although reliable and predictable preschool schedules are recommended, they cannot be set in stone—they must be flexible enough to accommodate unexpected changes. Despite our best efforts, sometimes the schedule just does not work; the children may be out of sorts for some reason, so making them adhere to a firm time frame can be harrowing and unproductive. Some days, we just need to be open to change and follow the flow.

Once, I tried to read a book to my group. As I opened the cover, a little hand shot up in the air. I called on her and she eagerly volunteered that her "Gramma was bringing her strawberry ice cream." I listened, acknowledged what she said, and then tried to return to the story. Within a microsecond, another hand shot up and the process repeated itself. Before long, every child wanted a turn to tell me something. I could have refused and doggedly tried to read the story, but instead I relented and put the book aside. The group wanted time to talk, so I gave it to them.

That was a valuable learning opportunity for me. Although I was the one "in charge," I had to remind myself that the day was not planned for me; it was planned for the children. I had already graduated preschool. They had not, so I was there for *them*. Since little children change like the wind, I needed to change, too.

A good classroom should have a little chaos running through it. Allow passion to enter the experience and let children be emotionally and actively engaged in what they are doing. Over the gentle hum of learning, it is good to hear an occasional crash in the block corner, shouts of joy when the papier-mâché volcano shoots vinegar and baking soda lava, and cymbals clash in the music center. Giggles should emanate from dramatic play, and every once in a while teachers should race children with gluey fingers to the sink. This *is* a functional classroom. Giving children the chance to learn something on their own is powerful. They are the "doers," the "actors," and the "learners."

FIGURE 7.1. Examples of Preschool Daily Schedules—
Half-Day, Full-Day, and Extended-Day Programs

Half-Day Program* (3 Hours)
8:45 a.m. Arrival—Children and parents are greeted at the door
8:45 a.m.–9:45 a.m. Free Play—All centers open
9:45 a.m.–9:55 a.m. Cleanup Time
9:55 a.m.–10:15 a.m. Morning Meeting—Welcome Song, Story, Group Share Time
10:15 a.m.–10:25 a.m. Bathroom time (as needed), Wash hands for snack
10:25 a.m.–10:40 a.m. Snack—Time for Conversation or Story
10:40 a.m.–10:50 a.m. Wash Hands—Bathroom time (as needed)
10:50 a.m.–11:20 a.m. Outdoor/Gross-motor Play
11:20 a.m.–11:30 a.m. Wash Hands—Bathroom time
11:30 a.m.–11:40 a.m. Group meeting—Story
11:40 a.m.–11:45 a.m. Get ready for pickup
11:45 a.m. Dismissal

Full-Day Program* (6 Hours)
8:30 a.m. Arrival—Children and parents are greeted at the door
8:30 a.m.–9:30 a.m. Free Play—All centers open
9:30 a.m.–9:40 a.m. Cleanup Time
9:40 a.m.–9:55 a.m. Morning Meeting—Welcome Song, Story, Group Share Time
9:55 a.m.–10:05 a.m. Bathroom time (as needed), Wash hands for snack
10:05 a.m.–10:20 a.m. Snack—Time for Conversation or Story
10:20 a.m.–10:30 a.m. Wash Hands—Bathroom time (as needed)
10:30 a.m.–11:30 a.m. Free Play—All centers open
11:30 a.m.–11:40 a.m. Cleanup Time (Bathroom time for those who require it)
11:40 a.m.–12:10 p.m. Outdoor/Gross-motor time
12:10 p.m.–12:20 p.m. Wash Hands—Bathroom time (as needed)
12:20 p.m.–12:50 p.m. Lunch
12:50 p.m.–1:00 p.m. Wash Hands/Bathroom time/Cot setup
1:00 p.m.–2:20 p.m. Nap/Rest Time
2:20 p.m.–2:30 p.m. Wake up/Bathroom Time
2:30 p.m.–2:40 p.m. Group story
2:40 p.m.–2:45 p.m. Get ready for pickup
2:45 p.m. Dismissal

PUTTING OUT MATERIALS THAT MAXIMIZE LEARNING

Classroom materials can make or break a preschool program. Having many items on hand is one thing; using them to effectively stimulate learning is another. If children do not have fun and interesting materials that promote exploration, discovery, and learning, then they won't be engaged.

Play is the work of childhood. Young children learn about the world through their interaction with it. They need to manipulate items to learn. Center-based programs offer a variety of choices and are ideal for children

FIGURE 7.1. (continued)

Extended-Day Program* (9 Hours)

8:30 a.m. Arrival—Children and parents are greeted at the door
8:30 a.m.–9:30 a.m. Free Play—All centers open
9:30 a.m.–9:40 a.m. Cleanup Time
9:40 a.m.–9:55 a.m. Morning Meeting—Welcome Song, Story, Group Share Time
9:55 a.m.–10:05 a.m. Bathroom time (as needed), Wash hands for snack
10:05 a.m.–10:20 a.m. Snack—Time for Conversation or Story
10:20 a.m.–10:30 a.m. Wash Hands—Bathroom time (as needed)
10:30 a.m.–11:30 a.m. Free Play—All centers open
11:30 a.m.–11:40 a.m. Cleanup Time (Bathroom time for those who require it)
11:40 a.m.–12:10 p.m. Outdoor/Gross-motor time
12:10 p.m.–12:20 p.m. Wash Hands—Bathroom time (as needed)
12:20 p.m.–12:50 p.m. Lunch
12:50 p.m.–1:00 p.m. Wash Hands/Bathroom time/Cot setup
1:00 p.m.–2:30 p.m. Nap/Rest Time
2:30 p.m.–2:40 p.m. Wake up/Bathroom Time
2:40 p.m.–2:55 p.m. Group story
2:55 p.m.–3:05 p.m. Bathroom Time
3:05 p.m.–3:40 p.m. Outdoor/Gross-motor Time
3:40 p.m.–3:50 p.m. Wash Hands—Bathroom time (as needed)
3:50 p.m.–4:55 p.m. Free Play—All centers open
4:55 p.m.–5:05 p.m. Cleanup Time (Bathroom time for those who require it)
5:05 p.m.–5:20 p.m. Group story
5:20 p.m.–5:30 p.m. Get ready for pickup
5:30 p.m. Dismissal

*Timing is flexible and subject to change, if needed.

at varying ages and levels of skill and competency. Although materials will be covered in much greater depth in the subsequent chapter, suffice it to say that children should have access to puzzles, fine-motor and small building materials, blocks, and dramatic play items. In addition, art supplies and resources for learning about science and nature, math, and numbers should be on hand. Lastly, books and materials that support writing and drawing should be available.

A good rule of thumb is to provide enough varied materials so all children have a choice, with some extras to spare. Then children can find something they like, play with it, and then move to something new when they lose interest. All materials should be accessible—that is, easy to reach and easily available, so don't overload the shelves. Like items should be stored together in marked bins and be easy to find. Shelves should not be jam-packed with toys and/or supplies, but should be relatively open, with materials arranged for quick viewing and easy access.

When we offer many varied materials, children choose what interests them most and explore them in their own personal way. Children are curious by nature and love to see new things. New items are like magnets to small children, so why not put them out and attract them?

Lastly, be sure to have enough of a single item to support the play of multiple children at one time. For instance, in a classroom of young threes, a child in the dramatic play area picked up a phone and pretended to talk to Daddy, prompting three others to do the same thing. There were a number of phones in the area (e.g., pretend cell phones, disconnected receivers, even a PVC pipe elbow joint), so no one had to fight over them.

However, three additional children came over to play, and then there were not enough phones to accommodate them. The teacher, realizing the situation and the value of pretend play, immediately picked up a block and modeled using it as a phone. The whole group, even those with phones, raced over and everyone started talking into "blocks." Luckily, there were more than enough blocks. The moral of the story: Have enough of an item to support play and learning and have the materials easily accessible to the children.

SETTING UP MEANINGFUL ACTIVITIES FOR SMALL GROUPS

Once the daily schedule is defined and the appropriate materials are selected, preschool teachers need to fill the time that is not devoted to personal care routines with fun and stimulating learning and social opportunities. Some time each day should consist of teacher-facilitated learning so two to four children can come together at a table or in a center and have a teacher introduce a concept and/or skill.

When done well, more occurs here than just directed learning. Ideas are advanced and supported with opportunities to work with materials and further explore them. Children are able to receive new information and expand their vocabulary. They are able to define and share their own thoughts with the group and learn that they have value. They learn to be considerate and cooperate with others.

A teacher can play games with a few children to familiarize them with taking turns and/or following directions, or model how to write a letter or number on paper. She might ask questions during a sink or float experiment, or work on a floor puzzle with a couple of children. The range of possibilities is extensive, but the objective is singular—to provide a child with a new learning possibility that instills a love of learning and then lets him or her take it to the next level of understanding.

THE VALUE OF FREE PLAY IN THE LEARNING PROCESS

Children learn best through their own direct, open-ended experience. Teachers do not have to be directly involved for discovery to occur. In fact, too much routine teacher involvement can stunt independent learning because children come to rely on the teacher to show them how to do something rather than doing it on their own. Passive learning does not always yield the best results.

Engaging in free play is an ideal way for children to identify areas that interest them and then experience them firsthand. Play is so important to the learning process, because children are busily learning new skills and concepts that are not readily apparent. Much more is happening when children enjoy free-choice time than one might imagine.

While exercising their free choice options, children are developing their thinking and planning skills, acquiring firsthand experience, and learning how to cooperate and interact with others. Furthermore, they are organizing their thoughts and experiences into a hierarchy that they can use at later points for reference and context. They are strengthening their language skills, developing conversation skills, and learning how to express themselves effectively with peers and adults.

Remember that we orchestrate the classroom, but the children vibrate the strings. Make materials, activities, and learning experiences available on a regular basis, so that children can touch them, explore them, and discover their power through them.

MAKING THE MOST OF CLEAN-UP TIME

In some preschool classrooms, clean-up time can be exasperating. It does not have to be. An effective teacher can turn the process around and make it a positive learning experience for the group. Aside from giving ample warning for clean-up and playing some music as a cue, teach responsibility and respect during the routine.

First, use clean-up time as a chance to teach children personal responsibility. When children take materials off the shelf and use them for work and play, they should replace them when they are done so another child can use them. Some people would say this is nearly an impossible lesson for a young child to learn, but it is not. Many Montessori preschool programs effectively teach this to children as young as 3.

Next, through the clean-up routine, teach the children to respect the classroom toys and materials. Explain to them that when they put materials away with care, they last longer.

Apply this practice to books as well. When replacing a book on the shelf, have the child return it with the cover facing forward and upright, spine to the left, so the books look inviting and attractive. Ask children to help fix the books when they are tossed haphazardly on a shelf (e.g., upside-down, sideways, or with the back cover showing) and then thank them for being so caring and cooperative. By doing this, we teach children that "books are our friends." Hopefully, it will prompt them to be careful, treat books well, and respect books more.

Follow the same practice in the block area. A neat block area has a distinct appeal, so make it easy for children to replace blocks neatly and arrange them by type and size. Affix small, permanent templates to the shelves to guide and encourage the children to put the correct type and sized block in its proper place. Also, have bins available for like-object accessories (e.g., people, animals, cars, trucks). When the block area is neat and organized, children learn respect and responsibility and the area invites children to play and build with care and attention. Maintain a neat block area, not a muddle.

When teachers explain that toys and books are important and should be respected, children learn valuable lessons about respecting property, which helps build character and enhance social relationships.

CAPITALIZING ON LARGE-GROUP MEETING TIME

The last daily routine to cover is the large-group meeting or circle time. At minimum, preschools should offer one large-group meeting; many have two and sometimes three, depending on the length of the day. Some use different meeting times for distinct purposes, such as to read a story, to enjoy music and movement, to review general information, and/or to introduce concepts.

It is worth mentioning that group size and age should be taken into account when children are sitting for long periods of time. Younger children should have shorter large-group experiences than older children, due to their shorter attention span and their propensity for squirming and poking one another when bored.

If the group size is particularly large, the group should be split into two or three smaller groups for circle and story time. If two teachers can cover the same general information with a smaller group, it is often beneficial, for there is more time for the group members to talk and share information. When a child has to wait for 18 other children to speak before it is her turn, she is likely to grow impatient. Use the time wisely and make it work for all involved. More learning can be accomplished when we divide and conquer.

Reviewing Classroom Rules

It is always a good use of time to review classroom rules and expectations during at least one meeting each day. Most programs do this at morning meeting because it helps set the tone for the rest of the day. When children can recall and recount the classroom rules, the rules are fresh in their minds. When teachers ask children how they can follow the rules, it allows those who regularly follow them to provide options for those who need help.

Teachers can create a very productive classroom system by putting the rules in positive terms. Rather than saying, "No running in the classroom," the rule can say, "We always use walking feet inside." Some programs take the display of the rules one step further and put them up in picture form. In addition, they supplement them with a pictorial consequence.

For example, two rules are presented: "We walk inside" and "We run outside." The teacher asks the children to walk and she takes a photo. She asks some to run inside and takes another photo. She takes a third photo of children running outside. To associate a clear expectation with a social response, she takes exaggerated photos of herself or other classroom teachers either smiling or frowning.

Then, she displays the picture rules and consequences. A picture of the children walking in the classroom is followed by a picture of happy teacher. A picture of the children running inside is coupled with a photo of a frowning teacher. The picture of children running outdoors is paired with a happy teacher photo. Children clearly understand these rules.

As children learn and master each rule, morning meeting can be used to acknowledge the successful learning of the rule and retire it. Children love to see the rules go away. Of course, put up another one in its place to set a new behavioral goal. Remember to grow the rules with the group.

Establishing a Community

Start each morning meeting with a welcome song, so the group greets each child by name and welcomes him or her into the bigger community. Also use this forum to share "big news" with the group, such as the birth of a new brother or sister. Involve the children in one another's lives, forge bonds of friendship, and create a community each day.

Introducing Concepts

Some programs use music to present and review information, and teachers sing songs such as "There are 7 days in a week" and "The months of the year" to review calendar information, "This Old Man" to review numbers and counting, and the "ABC" song to recite the alphabet.

In addition, teachers may ask a question and list the children's responses to model writing or create a graph to show numbers. Teachers might ask questions about the letter or theme of the week and get feedback from the children.

Some teachers use the meeting time to introduce the weather to the children and then appoint a "meteorologist" to look out the window and report what is happening outside. Based on the response, children might place corresponding felt pieces (e.g., the sun, clouds, snowflakes) on a flannel board.

Presenting a Story Book—Sharing Personal Stories

At least once, preferably twice a day, a book should be shared with the group in one form or another: A teacher can read a story, a child can share a story by interpreting the pictures, or a story CD and book can be presented. Once a story is shared, invite children to discuss the subject matter or share personally relevant stories, or read up to the last few pages of a story and then ask the children to create a new ending.

Teachers can direct the conversation toward specific learning goals. They can ask questions that prompt specific answers, such as "Who draws the pictures for a book?" Or they might ask open-ended questions that elicit broader responses.

Lastly, children can re-enact a story by becoming the characters, which makes learning fun and fosters self-expression and language exchange.

Enjoying Music or Movement

Sometimes, the group can come together to sing or dance informally, a specialist might visit the class and offer a guided music experience, or a teacher might take out instruments and lead a band around the room. While in a large-group context, teachers should sing songs, recite rhymes, and engage children in finger plays.

Posing a Question for Exploration

In the large-group forum, begin a learning opportunity with a question and have the children hypothesize about it before moving to active exploration and discovery. For example, ask what colors can be mixed to get a different color and then escort children over to the art table to find out. Or ask children to postulate what a magnet will attract and then give them a magnet and have them find out if they're right.

Teachers can facilitate learning by asking the right questions to the right children and seeing where the questions take them. The trick is having the right questions for each child.

Discussing Center Options and Outlining the Daily Plan

Before children leave the group and move into their own pursuits, review with them all of the centers so they know where they can go. Furthermore, identify activities that are offered in the centers so they can formulate a plan for their own learning. Facilitate each child's planning by asking where he or she would like to go and what he or she plans to do there.

Preschool teachers influence what transpires each day. By aptly utilizing the daily social routines, thoughtfully presenting materials and preparing the space, and optimizing learning opportunities, teachers can create and augment wonderful preschool experiences.

8

Creating the Optimal Center-Based Preschool Classroom

A center-based curriculum provides for all areas of human development: social, emotional, physical, language-based, and cognitive skill. In a center-based program, the teacher serves as a guide and facilitator rather than as an imposing central figure in the classroom. This format is ideal for children who are at varying ages and levels of skill and competency, and it enables teachers to customize a program that benefits individual children.

A center-based curriculum provides for skill mastery as well as new opportunities for learning. Children who engage in center-based learning are able to focus on the areas of knowledge they find most interesting, gratifying, and meaningful.

A center-based curriculum enables the teacher to tailor the program to the unique features of the group, include each child's cultural and ethnic heritage, and showcase diversity and multicultural ideas for all to see and share. Lastly, teachers greatly benefit from this learning style because they are able to keep the curriculum fresh and new for themselves and for the children, and they can get to know each child as a unique individual.

DEFINING THE SPACE WITH OPEN-OPTION LEARNING CENTERS

By setting up the different areas/centers in a way that can be frequently changed or augmented over the school year, the teacher is able to create a progressive learning environment.

Make a variety of centers open and available to the children every day, including a puzzle place, a fine-motor area, a writing center, an art area, a housekeeping (dramatic play) corner, a book nook, a cozy corner for quiet time, a listening center, a block corner, a discovery space (for math/number and science/nature exploration), a place for sensory play, and a music center. A computer area can be provided, but is not necessary. Every center should be replete with interesting and stimulating materials.

This chapter will focus on materials that are accessible in the different centers. The next chapter will discuss solid teaching practices that can support children's learning through their use.

A PUZZLE PLACE

Puzzles promote thinking, reasoning and problem solving using a very concrete format. Children are able to see *form* in a new way—they can see parts in relation to the whole, can integrate parts to make a larger picture, and can comprehend spatial relationships in this context. Puzzles provide the opportunity for children to demonstrate their competence to themselves and to others, develop self-confidence, and foster independence.

Place a variety of puzzles in a center and/or throughout the room. Since children grow and develop at their own rates, the puzzles should reflect different ages (knobbed and simple form) and levels of skill (9-piece or 12-piece framed pictures, floor puzzles) and ability, and should grow with the children. As children master one puzzle type, bring out new ones so they can continue to be challenged.

THE ART CENTER

Arts and crafts have a special significance to young children because this is where they are most self-expressive. In this setting, they use their imagination to make brand-new things—often never seen before by anyone. Here, they get a real sense of personal pride and accomplishment. They can make wonderful products or learn about themselves through the process.

> **Point**—Puzzles enhance hand-eye coordination and allow a child to engage in trial-and-error learning. Children learn basic math skills when building puzzles, such as the concepts of shape, size, color, similarity, difference, and location. They see relationships between form and background by filling in the holes. Lastly, when puzzle pieces are mixed up, children learn to sort and discriminate by type.

If possible, provide two art areas for the children. One should be open for much of the day and stocked with the basics for spur-of-the-moment creativity, such as materials for drawing and coloring, cutting and gluing, and modeling (e.g., play dough). In addition, have another, larger art area containing easels and tables that can accommodate two or more children engaged in messy personal discovery and open-ended creative self-expression. Children should be able to access a wide variety of materials independently.

Supply the art area with white and colored paper as well as crayons, markers, pencils, glue sticks, and glue. Collage materials (e.g., crinkle paper, feathers, sequins) or old magazines and scissors for cutting up new collage materials should be available in addition to items that have different textures (e.g., soft, fluffy, rough, smooth) and attributes (e.g., bright, shiny, dull, coarse). Clay and/or play dough should be offered routinely, as should wood-working materials (e.g., small pieces of wood, glue, clamps to hold the piece together). See Figure 8.1.

Set up an easel where individual paintings can be made and stock it with large paper and brightly colored paints. Vary the painting implements (e.g., sponges, brushes, rollers) to provide different experiences. When a child paints at the easel, his or her hand-eye coordination, which will be used later for reading and writing, is enhanced, and his or her

---

FIGURE 8.1. Typical Materials for Process Art Experiences

Collage: A free-form art piece compiled from a variety of materials

    Collages can be made using different textures (e.g., silk, burlap, tissue paper, sand paper, etc.); objects (e.g., Styrofoam peanuts, buttons, beads, wiggly eyes, etc.); colors and/or pictures (e.g., magazine photos, tissue paper, crinkle wrap, curly paper, etc.) and/or various diverse and colorful materials (e.g., curling ribbon, sequins, ripped colored paper, etc.).

Clay: Three-dimensional free-form creations using clay or another modeling product, completed at one time or over a few days

    Sometimes, the end result is kept; other times the focus was just on the experience of working with the medium. When an alternate modeling product is used (e.g., play dough), additives (scents—vanilla, lemon extracts, etc.; texture—sand or rice; or color—food dyes) extend the molding experience.

Woodworking: A wooden structure or conglomerate piece created from small wooden pieces

    Variations on this include using Styrofoam pieces in lieu of wood and golf tees in place of nails.

Goop and/or slime: A substance concocted of cornstarch, water, and/or glue, which can be used for messy play and/or scientific discovery

> **Point**—When offering play dough, occasionally add new textures to it, such as rice or sand, or add new scents, such as vanilla or lemon.

gross-motor movements become better controlled over time. While at the easel, children express their feelings through their choice of color; discover symmetry, balance, and design through their artwork; and learn about the relationship between size and space when filling a paper.

While engaging in tabletop art experiences with glue or finger paint, children learn about different textures and their personal tolerances for these messy experiences. They learn about color, shape, location, pattern, and design as they create their own unique artwork.

Lastly, offer children a soft dough or clay to massage, mold, and model.

THE FINE-MOTOR AREA

Fine-motor materials can build confidence and competence, so children gravitate to this area when they feel proficient in these tasks. Provide ample materials and a space where two to four children can engage in focused, individual work or come together to work as a team. Stock a shelf unit with a variety of manipulatives and small building materials. If a larger group of children is in the class, have even more on hand.

Manipulatives are those materials that require eye-hand coordination and some dexterity when joining or using them. These would include beads for stringing, lacing cards, plastic links, pegs and boards, shape sorters, and "potato heads." Usually, these can be stored easily in labeled bins and can be kept together in one place for easy access.

> **Point**—Manipulatives can be used to teach skills, such as putting a string through the hole in a bead and/or following a left-to-right progression, or to introduce concepts, such as patterning, sorting, and classifying by size or color, and/or one-to-one correspondence.

> **Point**—Small building materials can facilitate problem solving as children learn how to connect different objects to form the desired whole. When these items are used in small groups, children learn to express their needs and ideas, plan, and cooperate.

Small building materials link or connect to yield a larger work product, and may include DUPLOs, LEGOs, Lincoln logs, ringamajigs, K'nex, erector sets, or daisy, clown, or bunny builders. Having a variety of small building toys is recommended. Consider having three to five different types of building materials on hand. They can be distributed throughout the room and supplement various centers.

THE WRITING CENTER

Each classroom should have a designated writing center where children can draw, write, and learn to manage and maneuver a writing implement using their hand-eye coordination. Place it away from the noisier areas of the classroom, allowing for greater concentration.

Initially, writing skills are limited and children just scribble on their papers. However, as they physically grow, they learn to operate their hands with greater precision and are able to manage their pencil with greater skill. As their understanding of language develops, children learn to write letters and then words. Writing empowers children because they can skillfully maneuver a pencil or crayon, and convey their thoughts and ideas to others. Providing a writing center to children is like handing them the world in a pencil. It makes them *want* to express themselves.

A simple rule of thumb is: The more writing materials, the better. Aside from paper that a child can easily access, offer stubby or regular crayons and pencils, markers, colored pencils, dry-erase boards, and the corresponding markers and/or inkpads and stamps. Beyond the basics, add Post-it notes, envelopes, index cards, fancy stationery, old cards, and colored writing paper. A roll of tape (clear or colored) is always good, as are blunt-end scissors and glue sticks. In addition, put word cards, letter stencils, and other templates for writing as well as the children's journals so they can add to them. At least two chairs should be available.

A PUPPET CORNER

Provide puppets and a theater for the children to use. They can be handmade puppets or purchased from a store. Offer a variety, including soft animals, sock puppets, and character or people puppets. Sometimes mittens with eyes are sufficient.

Puppetry allows children to take on the role of another, experiment with different voices and tones, and fully engage their imagination. Puppets help children find their voice and use their words.

> **Point**—In addition to hand puppets, create shadow puppet plays. Place a sheet up on the wall, shine a bright light on it, and make finger puppet shadows. Have the children do it, or have them make up a story to describe what they see.

Children love to use puppets to put on shows. Granted, a story line is rarely followed. Usually, it is nothing more than free play with an audience, which often devolves into slapstick humor once a giggle is heard from the audience. Yet puppets serve a grander purpose by allowing the typically quiet child to have a voice.

In addition to serving as a bridge to language development and literacy, puppets allow a teacher to gain insight into the inner workings of a child. Puppets enable self-expression when a child feels self-conscious. When a youngster has had a tough day, a teacher can learn about the problem by giving him a puppet and asking the puppet questions. The typical 3- or 4-year-old will divulge a great deal more through his puppet than he or she would if questioned directly.

THE "HOUSEKEEPING CORNER"

Dramatic play is directly linked to imaginative play, and in this area the play is always rich and creative, so it is often popular. While here, children can assume new roles, pretend to be different people, or just work out questions they have about the bigger social world—all in relative safety. Having a place to experiment with different life situations can be very beneficial to young children.

Instead of having just a standard housekeeping corner, change it to give it new life. Embellish the space and add props that are appealing. Create prop boxes (e.g., shoe store, animal hospital, post office, restaurant) and bring them out throughout the year. By providing for different play scenarios, the dramatic play area can open up new points for class discussion (e.g., places in the neighborhood such as the bakery or community helper roles such as police officer). Within a single month, children can be a veterinarian, an astronaut, a restaurant owner, and a "baby" while playing house.

What kinds of props should be in the dramatic play area? First and foremost, familiar furnishings that promote role-play—often house play. Many programs have a kitchen area and doll furniture for playing

> **Point**—Dramatic play encourages children to express themselves verbally, try out different adult roles, solve social problems with peers through negotiation, and play interactively using symbolic representation.

"house." In addition, have props for career-related props (a doctor's kit, a cash register, a tool kit, computer keyboards) to promote "work" play for both boys and girls. Add ancillary props such as plastic food, dishes, pots and pans, telephones, dolls, and baby care items.

If the children are engaged in dress-up games, then there should be enough clothing available so everyone has a choice. For instance, if there are four children allowed in that area at any one time, then there should be six or seven different outfits from which to choose. Also, there should be ample items to pick from for both boys and girls. Often, the dress-up clothes are slanted toward the girls, but boys like to dress up as well, so have things available for them, too.

What kinds of dress-up clothes should be available? Shirts for men and women, dresses, skirts, shoes, scarves, hats, purses, wallets, old costumes, and maybe some of those pullover dress-up "vests." Ask parents for donations from home, such as old clothes they find during spring cleaning. Children tend to like those items the most. Other children prefer simple scarves made from squares of fabric purchased at local craft stores.

Reflect the diversity of the world, with multicultural dolls and foods representative of different cultures and ethnicities, but do not have stereotypical clothes. Then everyone can play without exception or exemption.

THE BOOK NOOK

Each classroom should have a book nook or library corner filled with books. There should be a variety of books ranging in topics, from fairy tales and cute animal stories to nonfiction books to books about foreign places to books about science, nature, and numbers. Books that familiarize children with special needs, such as autism, hearing loss, and visual impairment, among others, should be represented, too.

The book nook affords children tremendous information. Books help make sense of the big and confusing world. Books describe new situations, explain familiar ones, and give children words to use when expressing themselves. Books show new places and describe different worlds and experiences. Books open the imagination.

> **Point**—Books help children understand the connection between written and spoken words, between illustrations and actual objects. By hearing stories read, children develop more complex language and speech patterns, expand their vocabulary, and broaden their knowledge of the world. Experience with books enables children to recognize words and eventually sight-read. Finally, a well-written book supports a love of reading and a well-illustrated one fosters an appreciation for art.

In addition to opening the mind, books can calm the spirit. Reading a book to children can help settle them down and refocus their attention and interest. Reading a book can open group discussion or set the stage for imaginative play. Looking at the pictures in a book can add new visual experiences and foster more questions.

Why offer a book nook? Every child at one point in the day needs a place to go to take a break, so the space should be conducive to resting and relaxing with a book. It is not a place for active play.

What should be available in a book nook? A cozy chair, comfortable pillows, or bean bags will help a child settle in and read or look at books. Books should be kept there and rotated frequently in connection with classroom themes or variations in the lesson plans. Books of varying levels should be kept on bookshelves in that space.

THE COZY CORNER

A cozy corner is a quiet place for rest and relaxation. Sometimes it is a quiet space with a game or activity set up for two children, a thinking chair for one, or a small tent or box designated for calming down.

Offer a cozy corner that has clean, comfortable cushions. Add some soft toys; simple activities, such as a puzzle or some lacing cards; and a few books so a tired child will use it to regroup. Or provide a listening center with an easy-to-operate tape player and book/tape sets.

> **Point**—Model how to take a break to the children by sitting in the space and looking at a book. Everyone needs a break during the day—even young children!

> **Point**—When children build block towers, they feel competent.
> When they construct cities and move the little figures around, they feel
> empowered. When they tower over their creations, they feel big, and that's
> quite a change for a young child.

THE BLOCK CORNER

Every early childhood classroom should have a block area where children can develop pre-math and pre-science skills. This center is a great place to put their emerging technical skills to work. In the block area, children learn how to measure, estimate, put things together, and take things apart. They also have firsthand experience with gravity. But that is not all—they also learn to work together, negotiate, communicate, and plan projects with visible outcomes. Most important, they learn that they can create, build, plan, and learn through trial and error without real repercussions.

The block area should be spacious enough so three or four children can converge, spread out, and build independent structures. An ample supply of varied blocks should be accessible, including wooden unit and view-through blocks, smaller shaped and colored wedges, child-created ones (made from donated oatmeal containers or cereal boxes), and platform and/or cardboard blocks. Provide ample accessories, such as people, animals, cars/trucks, and even dinosaurs, for independent play, so that grabbing and whining are kept to a minimum.

In addition, the block area should have a low-pile carpet or floor area suitable for building. Use sound-absorbing materials here, since the sound of crashing blocks can be disruptive. The space should be out of the way so no one has to walk through it to access another area in the room. It should also be separated from the quieter learning pursuits such as the book nook, the listening center, the writing table, and the fine-motor/puzzle-building areas so as to not be distracting.

Books should be accessible here (even a few construction-specific books) to supplement play and planning. Some children use pictures in a book as a basis for making their structure; others will use a story as a starting point for building and play. One program even had actual architectural plans hanging on the wall above the block shelves.

THE DISCOVERY CENTER

The discovery center can combine math and number discovery with science and nature exploration. Children will gravitate to this area if it is well-stocked and motivating. In addition to putting out materials, set up exciting activities and experiments to attract the children.

Although math and number materials can be found throughout the room, have additional materials in the discovery area. Set out a variety of items that inspire learning about measurement (measuring tapes, rulers, measuring cups and spoons, pan balance scales, egg timers or kitchen timers, growth charts and a scale); color, shape, and size (memory games, shape sorters, geometric puzzles, nesting cups); number recognition (number charts, posters, cash register, pegs and boards); and counting (varied counters with trays for sorting and classifying, unifix cubes, dominoes). Puzzles can be included in the number recognition items, as can posters and books about numbers. There should be three to five items for each of these categories.

Vary the activities so children are intrigued by the different ways they can learn math. Offer games to play (e.g., lotto, dominoes) and puzzles with numbers or sequences to build. Have children use tweezers or tongs to sort colored pom-poms. Chart the growth of a bean plant. Turn over an egg timer and have them measure as many shoes as they can by using a measuring tape before the sand runs out. Weigh different objects using a two-pan balance. Play a version of "I Spy" where children have to find colors or shapes in the classroom. Sort varied buttons using an ice cube tray. Make a chain of patterned links, then measure how long the chain is and count the number of links it has. The possibilities are endless.

Items in the science and nature section can have the same impact on learning. Materials should include living things such as plants or goldfish; natural objects or collections, including shells, rocks, and pinecones; books, posters, and pictures that relate to nature or scientific concepts; simple experiments such as magnets, magnifying glasses, and float bottles; and varied activities such as a spider web to examine, objects to weigh with a scale, and "goop" made by the group that stimulate discovery.

THE SENSORY TABLE—SAND AND WATER

The sand/water table is a place for children to come together and play as a group or individually. Often, this place is where discovery and experimenting occur. Children watch what others are doing and imitate their actions or enjoy the process of pouring, measuring, sifting, or experiencing

> **Point**—When children work with water, they uncover new concepts such as how objects sink of float, how temperature can change the state of water, how water surface tension changes when you add liquid soap, and so on. When working with sand, children learn the concepts of full and empty, and see how volume and weight change when they shift sand between containers.

the different textures. This is also the place where children mingle with new friends and talk about the day's experiences. It is also a good place to go for quiet reflection and time away from the general activity. Children benefit from the presence of sand, water, or sensory play more than one may think.

Offer a sensory table large enough to accommodate a few children at one time. Alternate sand and water play. Extend the experience by changing the materials, such as ice cubes, snow, mud, gravel, or gelatin, or art materials such as torn paper, "goop," or clay. Sand and water play provide opportunities to experiment with both wet and dry media, and offer the chance to learn pre-math and pre-science lessons while getting wet and/or dirty.

THE OUTDOOR PLAYGROUND AND INDOOR GYM

The outdoor playground or an indoor gross-motor space is where children get to release their pent-up energy. Children should be able to get gross-motor activity at least once each day, preferably twice, if possible.

The outdoor play space should have both stationary and portable equipment, including a climber and child-sized slide, as well as balls, hoops, jump ropes, and so on.

Inside, a gross-motor space can have the same portable equipment as listed for outdoor use, as well as mats for tumbling, balance beams, climbing steps, and rocking boats. Riding toys can be used in both venues.

> **Point**—Children enhance their physical development when they engage in large-motor activity. In addition to self-confidence, they develop their physical strength, coordination, and balance.

> **Point**—The use of riding toys during gross-motor play allows children to expend their energy in constructive ways and helps them learn the concepts of speed, direction, and location.

THE MUSIC CENTER

The music/listening center invites children to move freely about the classroom, transition to different activities, and accomplish tasks, either as individuals or as a group. Music fosters creative self-expression and enhances language development and interpersonal communication. It also promotes memory skill and enhances verbal expression. Music unites a group, and encourages fine- and gross-motor activities. Music creates a context for dance and physical movement. It also makes being a child a lot of fun!

Incorporate a music center and have musical and rhythmic instruments, such as rhythm sticks, bells, sand blocks, cymbals, and triangles, accessible in an open bin on the floor or on a low shelf for easy access. Do not place them in closed cabinets or on inaccessible shelves. Provide scarves and other props to use for dance and free movement.

Materials are important to successful learning. Children need to have direct access to them so they can engage in active experiences and trial-and-error learning. When materials are coupled with inspiring and appealing activities, and facilitated by a talented teacher, then knowledge is not far behind.

Point—When children sing songs as a group, they enhance their language skills, expand their vocabularies, increase their memory skills, and learn the principles of music and rhythm. They also extend their knowledge of cultural music and dance. When they use rhythm instruments, they learn about rhythm, timing, and timbre as well as the concepts of fast and slow, loud and soft, and different pitches. When they enjoy dance and movement, they learn how to control their body movement, and use their bodies to interpret the music and its mood.

9

Optimizing the Center-Based Preschool Experience with Solid Teaching Practice

Once materials are set up, the real job begins. Teachers must facilitate the learning experience of all the children by capturing their interest, focusing their attention, and supporting their personal and social experiences. Be available to all children. Be present with each child. Be instrumental in the learning, but do not dominate the process. Plan a general activity to interest the group, but know how to engage each child.

FACILITATING THE ART EXPERIENCES

Before discussing teacher practices for art, let's first talk about preschool art experiences in general. Typically, two types of art experience are offered to preschoolers: product art and process art. A quick look around the classroom will indicate which type the teacher favors. If the artwork looks the same, is made from precut pieces prepared by the teacher, has a limited choice of materials, and is realistic rather than fantastical, it is product art. In contrast, if the display highlights individualized self-expression, more and varied materials are used, it has free form, is unique, and is open to interpretation, it is process art.

Product art is usually a teacher-directed project that has a final, intended outcome, likely associated with a weekly theme. Some teachers still plan a craft, create an example, and then have the children reproduce it. Over the years, this approach has fallen out of favor, mostly due to the emphasis on the Developmentally Appropriate Practice and Emergent Curriculum in early education.

Process art offers art experiences purely for creative self-expression. There is no expected outcome; instead, children create whatever they want by using an open array of materials. Typically, teachers use a process approach when setting up collage, clay, and/or woodworking experiences.

A combination of the two approaches can benefit young children. Occasionally, some art projects can be teacher-directed art activities, which result in a product and teach the children to follow directions and have an end goal in mind. However, resist offering only cookie-cutter art projects or predetermined experiences, for the true goal of an art experience should be creative self-expression. Encourage the children to make what *they* want so that art experiences are personally meaningful. Ideally, children should be able to create their own masterpiece whenever they visit the art table.

Consider the following example when offering art. One September, a teacher offered her preschoolers their first art project. Since the theme was apples, she had the group make apple trees. She made a model of an upright trunk covered across the top with a green cloud-like treetop randomly dotted with red stickers, and placed it on the table. She provided precut brown trunks, green clouds, and just red stickers for the apples, even though earlier that day, the children had identified apples as being either red, green, or yellow. She called some children over for art and five children came.

Two children followed her model exactly. A third child put the green cloud upright on the trunk rather than horizontally, she helped him fix it, and he walked away from the art table, crying. The fourth child made a smiley face using the apples on his tree; the teacher corrected him, making him randomly put the apples all over the treetop. After she changed his artwork, he grabbed his paper and ripped it up. The last child wanted the apples to fall in a straight line down to the ground, and the teacher tried to correct him. He declined to listen. Once he finished, she put his paper in his cubby to be taken home, and did not hang it up. The only two pictures she displayed were the ones that looked like hers. That was striking. Why not display inventiveness and creativity? Why prize only conformity? Why not let the children decide on the colors for the tree trunk, the apples, and the leaves? Why not let them arrange the items any way they want? They have a lifetime of conformity ahead of them; why not splurge on creativity now?

PRACTICE AND PUPPETS

Making puppets and using them in the classroom opens up a whole new world to children, especially those who may be shy or afraid to voice their opinions or feelings, so set up a center where children can create their own puppets.

Create a mystique around puppetry. Encourage children to use puppets to tell their own stories or replicate one they know from a book. Create a puppet theater for the children to use, have them decorate it, and place a curtain on it that opens and closes. Link their show to the written word by writing out their story as it unfolds, and, at a later point, have them illustrate it and keep it as a storybook for the class.

SUPPORTING DRAMATIC PLAY

Dramatic play is synonymous with imaginative play. This open-ended center can be used to enhance language skills, engage in creative and cooperative play opportunities, enable children to try on different family roles, and define a stronger sense of self and a greater understanding of others. Depending on how a teacher uses the space, dramatic play can support the various themes the teacher would like to cover in the course of a year.

Furthermore, dramatic play can be augmented in unique ways by introducing new items, for they can lead play in a whole new direction and yield a great deal of learning. Consider the story of the donated wok.

The teacher showed the group a wok at circle time and asked them to tell her what it was. Initially, they decided it was a crown, so one child placed the ring and wok bowl on his head, but it fell off. Next, they hypothesized that it was a hat, flipped the bowl over, and tried to wear it, but it slipped off. Finally, a timid girl told the group it was a *wok*, a cooking tool that her mother used at home.

The teacher asked her to show how it is used, so she put all the pretend food from housekeeping into it and stirred it quickly. Soon everyone wanted to try, and before long, the whole group was playing excitedly with it. For the rest of the week, the group was inspired to learn more about Chinese cooking and food, so housekeeping was transformed into a Chinese restaurant, complete with takeout menus and child-made decorations. The teacher bought sticky white rice, fried rice, and brown rice to taste, and graphed taste preferences as a math activity. Novel learning can result from a simple change to the dramatic play area. Never underestimate the power of a wok.

Some teachers have perfected the art of linking centers to specific classroom themes or new concept areas. Although this takes additional time and planning, it often proves fruitful when an idea can be extended throughout the classroom and across time. For example, creating some props for the dramatic play area can make the play more fun or turn a fun day of play (e.g., being astronauts, complete with paper bag helmets and a cardboard box rocket) into a classroom book, written and illustrated by the group.

BOLSTERING BLOCKS

Block play supports the development of pre-math and pre-science skills, so be inventive with blocks and accessories to promote that type of learning. Why not require children to perform actual math functions upon entering and leaving the block area?

Place a four-unit block (i.e., the really long one) at the entrance to the center. Mark it off so children can clearly see that four units of blocks make up the long block, and use this as a device to show that only four children can be in the center at one time. Next, affix the name and photo of each child to his or her own brick-sized quarter block. As children enter or exit the area, have them place their brick on, or remove it from, the long block. Teach them the word *add* when they go into the center, so they can say, "I added my block," and teach them the phrase *take away* when they leave, so they can say, "I am leaving and taking away my block." Before long, the children will discover that, when there are four blocks on the big block, no one else can come in, and they will be speaking in equations because they will be *living* it, not just learning it through rote instruction.

One final note regarding the block and dramatic play centers—keep them open and accessible. They are popular and produce a lot of necessary learning. By limiting access to them, you inadvertently create a higher demand. Open them often and for longer time periods, so children learn how to play there with little incident, learn to be responsible for cleaning the areas up, and become more familiar with the play opportunities they present. By giving the children easy and frequent access, these centers lose their luster. After the glow wears off, a center becomes less popular. Some children will gravitate to it, but others will not.

ENCOURAGING DISCOVERY

Incorporating science into the daily routine can be easy. During morning meeting, discuss the weather and talk about the changes that happen over time. During snowy months, conduct experiments using ice and snow; during warmer months, see how long it takes water to evaporate from an open jar. Year-round, do planting activities using seeds, bulbs, and pieces of vegetables.

Bring the natural world into the classroom by catching an ant and temporarily keeping it in a bug jar, by making a compost pile and adding earthworms, or by finding an extinct beehive for close examination. Have children directly interact with nature by watering the plants and feeding the fish, examining natural objects using magnifying glasses or microscopes, adding to the natural collection, or making mud. Enjoy nature outdoors by attracting and feeding birds with pinecones covered with bird seed or through taking a nature walk and focusing on different plants, flowers, animals, or insects. Encourage active connections with the natural world.

Involve the group in science and nature activities by bringing in tadpoles and watching them change into frogs, by observing butterflies transition from chrysalis to butterfly, or by creating papier-mâché volcanoes and making them erupt by mixing baking soda and vinegar. Combine science and art by making wings and become birds, add antennas and be bugs. When science comes alive in the classroom, it creates enthusiasm.

Cook with the children. Follow a recipe. Make butter by shaking a can filled with heavy cream, a pinch of salt, and marbles. Grow sugar crystals on string. Make new batches of play dough for the art area. Bake oatmeal cookies to show how new things can be made using different ingredients— the sum of the whole is yummier than its component parts.

Make science personal by focusing on the human body and the five senses. Unite math and science by recording the children's height and weight over time or by measuring and comparing the length of their feet. Do taste tests; chart their food preferences, such as spaghetti with butter or sauce or cheese. The possibilities are unlimited. Just remember that science is more than magnets.

SUPPORTING MUSIC

Play music in the classroom; it soothes the soul. A teacher can play a CD for the entire group or keep a child-friendly tape player on hand for individual listening. Play different types of music, such as classical composition, nature sounds, multicultural music, child-friendly rock or pop, instrumental jazz, R&B, or show tunes; don't limit selections to just children's music. Why? The reason is three-fold: First, this may be the only place children hear a variety of music; second, different types of music have different effects on the classroom mood; and finally, music can be coupled with fun movement activities.

Offer props to invite movement. For example, take a simple plastic slip-on bangle bracelet and tie curling ribbon to it. These simple additions can be a big hit with the group.

When things become too hectic in the classroom, put on New Age background music and teach the children simple guided meditation to help them settle down. Invite them to pretend they are on a beach: Have children put their towels on the floor, close their eyes, and rest on them as the teacher talks about the sound of the waves, the call of the gulls, the warm sun on their skin, and the cool breeze blowing over them. Help the children manage their stress, knock their energy level down a peg, and enhance their ability to focus when they return to "work" and play. This is a great stress-reliever and it gives a teacher some downtime as well.

Incorporate yoga into the daily routine by showing children a few simple poses that invite imagination and relate to their concrete experience. Flutter bent legs like butterflies, stretch like tired dogs, and arch backs like angry cats. Yoga helps young children cope with stress and frustration, and offers peaceful sanctuary within.

"Read" the children. Know when to employ a stress-reduction strategy and know how long to keep it going. Take the time that is necessary, do not rush them, and know when to stop and move on to something else. This is an important aspect of early childhood education—timing.

Best teaching practice always involves observation. Watch free play and capitalize on learning moments. Facilitate learning with one child and watch it spread like wildfire throughout the room. Create "mini-experts" by offering them time and repeated opportunities to master concepts, then encourage them to share what they have learned with others, both teachers and peers. This child-centered teaching approach can create a waterfall effect across the entire group and spur others to learn a concept as well.

Utilize an emergent learning framework so this can happen more readily. Allow open-ended child-initiated learning to occur daily, so one child's learning moment can shape the classroom plan for all.

Utilize all the centers so each child's talents and interests can be defined and developed, then observe where the children go and what they do so planning for each child becomes easier.

We all have skills that are special to us and are just waiting to be developed and shared. We just need to discover the "seed," nurture the "plant," and watch it blossom.

EXPERIENCING LITERACY

With the recent push toward literacy in early childhood, reading has become very important. Books foster a love for learning. Young children enjoy hearing stories and looking at pictures; they eagerly initiate contact with books. Books help children construct a frame of reference for life; they help create a context for understanding themselves and others.

Offer varied books, including those that encourage imagination and creative thinking (fiction and fantasy picture books), define new concepts (e.g., science, math), promote a deeper understanding of people (e.g., historical tales, different skill levels), and offer positive social role models that depict people from different backgrounds, genders, and age groups in prosocial ways. Keep the old favorites on hand, so children can return to them again and again.

Do not restrict stories to just the book nook or the quiet corner; have them in all centers. I have seen children request a story only to have the hope dashed because a teacher has to find a book or cross a child-filled room to sit with them. Many things can prevent willing readers from reading.

Vary the books in the centers. Have a few that relate to the center's activity, such as trucks and buildings in the block center, and add others for pure enjoyment and entertainment, such as fairy tales from foreign lands. Programs that prize literacy even have a traveling book basket that goes outside.

Place books at different heights. Do not just keep them on bookshelves or on top of shelf units. Have them in bins and baskets on the floor so they are easy to access.

Offer a range of books, such as picture-word associations, simple stories, and early readers, to supplement learning (e.g., weather, animals, dinosaurs, space and the planets, plants, marine life) and augment concept or skill development (e.g., counting and identifying number, color, shape, and size). Supply fantastical stories, classic fairy tales, and new variations on old themes. Borrow books from the public library. Find the same tale using different cultural viewpoints. Support the cultural heritage and practices of children and staff members with books.

Since some children come from non-English-speaking homes, offer books in their native language so they feel welcomed by them. When parents can see that their language is included, they become more invested in the program and in their child's education, which solidifies the relationship between the school and the home and between the teacher and the family.

Share stories of people living with challenging conditions (e.g., autism, sensory impairment, mental challenge) so children can better understand them. Illustrations should favorably show people using assistive technology such as braces, eyeglasses, wheelchairs, and audio adapters. By providing a glimpse into diverse life experiences, questions can be posed and answered, allowing children to understand, accept, and include one another.

Encourage children to write and illustrate their own stories and then staple them into a booklet and place them on the library shelf. Make class books after mastering a new concept (a book of shapes), special field trips (e.g., a visit to the firehouse), or fun lessons (e.g., butterfly transformation). Encourage individuals to create books as well.

Some programs invest a lot of time and effort in their libraries. Huge collections are organized by theme or content, enabling quick reference. Others have extensive lending libraries that encourage reading in the home. Of course, some books may be "checked out" by families for a long time, but it is worth the risk. When you realize that a book borrowed from school might be the only children's book at home, having it returned in a timely fashion—or at all—should be unimportant. After all, over the years, the classroom library has been supplemented with family donations and book sale proceeds. The net gain outweighs the occasional loss.

Creating a Literate Preschool Environment

Language does not emerge in a vacuum; it needs to be supported in the environment. Expose children to language in many ways by making word-object associations, engaging in conversation, teaching words in sign language, reading books, and playing music. Some children learn through listening and can remember what they have heard; others need to physically move in order to make a piece of information personal and permanent; still others use visual perception to make sense of the world and their knowledge. Thus, we need to provide a variety of language opportunities.

Children must hear language to replicate it. Model it with articulation and enthusiasm, so it can grab hold and take shape. Introduce words and expand vocabulary through books and music. Since hearing the spoken word is vital to successful language development, adults need to speak often to young children.

Promote the Exchange of Language

Before focusing on literacy per se, let's first talk about the roles of communication and self-expression. As often as possible, incorporate conversation into the daily routine and have "talk time" as a regular part of the circle meeting. Encourage the children to plan before starting a project or entering a play space, and define it in advance using whole sentences, such as "I would like to go to the block corner to make a city with the colored blocks." While working with materials, ask children questions and have them explain the choices they made. If they subsequently want to change their plan, let them, but first have them verbally formulate a new one. Always *listen* to what they say.

Throughout the day, have individual conversations with children, and get to know their personal likes and dislikes. Ask them "Why?" Encourage them to ask their own questions to adults and peers. Foster conversation within groups and between children. Teach them to listen to others as well as to express themselves. Have them tell imaginative stories when playing, writing, and drawing.

While in a large group, ask simple daily questions that can be easily answered. Chart each child's response on a dry-erase board. Let them see their words in written form. Do not ask only "yes/no" questions; ask open-ended questions, such as "How?" and "Why?" These require longer answers and more thinking.

Throughout the day, add pertinent information to extend the idea or plan, and verbally expand an experience by providing more descriptive or educational information. For example, if a child asks for "water," get it and say, "Here is some cold water. I put it in a plastic cup for you."

Whenever possible, expand children's vocabularies with new words. Talk to children about their activities, and describe what they are doing as they work so they can associate words with their actions. Give children chances to ask questions, so they can learn to clarify their thinking while in varying group situations and/or while working independently with teachers.

Assess children's thinking as they work. As a child draws a picture, ask what it is and why she chose certain colors. Or as he puts a puzzle together, ask how he knows where the next piece goes. Comment on children's work to prompt them to think or explain their ideas.

Give the children ample opportunities to interact and express themselves. Place props such as dolls and phones throughout the room to encourage verbal exchange; supplement the block area with little people, animals, and dinosaurs; and put games and simple experiments in the science and math areas to promote interaction.

Support Literacy and Pre-Reading

Teachers can promote language and literacy through a variety of activities. See Figure 9.1.

Let a child choose a book and "read" it aloud to another child, a teacher, or the group at circle time or during transitions. In the listening center, audiotape children as they tell stories about the pictures.

Encourage children to act out stories and nursery rhymes. Provide props (e.g., a spider, a cushion) for playacting and associate them with

FIGURE 9.1 Teacher-Directed Literacy Activities

Read to the children in large groups, small groups, and individually at least twice a day.

Ask the group a question of the day and write out their responses.

When writing words on the easel, have the children sound out each letter as you write it.

Let children take turns writing out words on the easel at meeting time.

Talk often to the children about their activity. Comment on their work or ask questions that prompt them to think or explain their ideas.

"Publish" class-made books that have been written and illustrated by the children.

Leave notes for the children in the different centers so they can be intrigued by the "mystery writing." Encourage them to sound out the note to make sense of it.

Read a story and then ask the children to make up a new ending for it. Write it down.

Cook with the group so that children can see a recipe being used and followed.

Create your own recipes for cooking.

Create shopping lists for the teacher or wish lists from which the parents can make donations.

---

stories that the children know (e.g., Little Miss Muffet). Or build a puppet theater where children can tell stories with the puppets.

As a special group activity, set up a performance stage, complete with a curtain, and invite children to entertain one another with a song, a story, a joke, or a dance. Make sure everyone has a turn, and remind everyone to clap when the performer finishes. This will heighten the performer's self-esteem, teach cooperation, and promote public speaking and/or verbal storytelling.

During circle time, play language games such as "Telephone," "I Spy," same letter, and/or rhyming games. Sing songs such as "Row, Row, Row Your Boat," then make up new lyrics—for example, "Drive, drive, drive the car, carefully down the street." Be creative and have fun!

Encourage children to talk about their own experiences at group time, and teach them how to take turns, listen, and be respectful. Introduce a "Mr. Chatty"—that is, a small object that a child holds during his or her turn—and explain that whoever has it is the only person allowed to speak. Once finished, ask the speaker to pass Mr. Chatty to the best listener. This process encourages and rewards attentive and respectful listening, and decreases shouting out or talking all at once.

When demonstrating a process or skill for the group, such as tying a shoe, speak out loud while performing the action, so children can once again link words to actions. When finished, ask the children to explain in their own words how to do it. Write out the sequence and ask questions to ascertain their level of understanding.

Involve the families in literacy activities. Invite them to check out books from the classroom lending library, and ask them to support their child's reading/writing skills by writing stories with them at home. A fun way to do this is to send a stuffed animal (and a notebook) home for a weekend adventure. When the toy returns, have the child read the story and show their illustrations to the group.

Promote Self-Expression Through Writing

Incorporate writing into the children's daily experience and play. Provide a writing center with writing instruments such as pencils, colored pencils, crayons, markers, stamps, and inkpads, chalk and chalkboards, and different kinds of paper, including white and colored paper, lined paper, envelopes, index cards, stationery, and Post-it notes. Include other fun desktop accessories, such as a tape dispenser, safe scissors, and glue sticks, to encourage a sit-down visit. Provide an alphabet strip, letter stencils, and templates as well as name and word cards to encourage letter and word writing. Visit the writing center often and help children build their skills. Show them by example how to write in a linear fashion. Demonstrate how to write upper- and lowercase letters, but keep the experience nonthreatening. Maintain good records of children's writing in a portfolio. Have children keep their own journals. These will be a great way to show each child's progress over time.

Display the children's writing samples. Designate a space for each child and let him or her choose what will be posted there. Always respect a child's work product. Never write the child's name or a description of the artwork directly on it; instead, write what children say on Post-it notes so they can peel them off and keep their work as they intended.

Make the environment print-rich: Place menus and magazines around so children see words; display recipes when cooking, or step-by-step procedures when doing science projects and refer to them so they link acting, thinking, and reading; hang word/object posters that help children make associations; and provide a name and word wall, organized alphabetically, with familiar words that children can recognize. Let the children add to it whenever they wish. Supplement the discovery center with photos of familiar objects, pictures of children performing experiments, and posters to show new concepts, such as sinking and floating.

In conclusion, teaching children to organize their thoughts, plan out their actions, and express themselves, both verbally and in writing, will set them on the path to success. In the big world, success is attained through effective communication.

Part III

THE EARLY CHILDHOOD EDUCATION EXPERIENCE:

Interpersonal Interactions

10

Creating Supportive Interpersonal Relationships in the Preschool

Many relationships are fostered in the preschool setting, including those between children, between adults, and most importantly, between teacher and children. Since our focus is on best teaching practice, we will attend to the teacher-child connection first and foremost, but we will also look at the ways a preschool environment can support the adults as well.

THE TEACHER-CHILDREN CONNECTION

When interacting with young children, treat them with respect, kindness, and empathy. Speak *with* a child; do not talk *at* them and do not talk *down* to them. All too often, adults command or direct rather than request or comment. They forget that young children deserve the same respect and kindness that adults would expect themselves. All people deserve to be treated well—young and old alike.

Children admire and revere adults. To small children, adults are all-knowing—they can get the knot out of the shoelaces without throwing a tantrum, fix the pedal on the tricycle, and know what words will help get the truck back from the child who just took it away. To children, adults know everything.

Thus, when an adult provides information or gives an opinion, children do not question it; they believe and readily accept it. Children learn about themselves through their conversations with adults, so use positive and productive statements.

Use Prosocial Proactive Speech

Children depend on adults to guide them, teach them, and provide information about the larger social world. As role models, adults lead the way, showing how to act, where to go, and what to say. Adults demonstrate what is possible and, hopefully, show children what is best. Since children are trusting, naive, and dependent, they believe what they are told, so adults should provide positive messages about them and the world.

Be kind in your interactions with children and teach them how to have caring relationships. Correct them when they act in unkind ways and help them adopt a different tone or response when speaking with peers. Keep in mind that they have learned how to act by watching others. Very few children are precocious enough to be malicious from within. Many have seen malicious behavior, stored it, and adopted it as their own. Offer alternatives to this choice by teaching respect, empathy, and prosocial choices for interaction.

Do not erode children's foundation with criticisms, by implying they are slow ("You are taking too long"), a poor listener ("How many times do I have to tell you?"), unruly ("Keep your hands to yourself and sit still!"), or disobedient ("Why can't you follow the rule like everyone else?"). Do not disable them with negativity, by harping on mistakes or poor choices they made; they are young and they are going to make poor choices.

Empower them through constructive and productive speech. Tell them when they have made a good choice, acknowledge when they follow the rules, and thank them when they help a peer. Have your speech be consistent with your goal for the children. For example, teach children respect by asking them to come over, rather than telling them to get up. Teach consideration by holding the door for them and letting them hold it for you. Teach empathy by asking them to comfort the friend they just hit rather than forcing them to say "I'm sorry." Help them express themselves by offering them a sentence such as, "Ask him to wait until your turn is finished," rather than saying, "Use your words." Children can always benefit from our guidance and direction.

Model Appropriate Behaviors

Take this idea to the next level and teach the children by example. Model what they should do. If the goal is to be polite and well-mannered, routinely say "please," "thank you," and "you're welcome."

Follow "the golden rule" in thought, word, and deed. Teach children to be kind to others so they will be kind back. It may sound trite, but it is a truism worth following. Choose constructive and encouraging words. Use sincere comments that build self-esteem. When a mistake is made, take responsibility so children can see how it is done. Be accountable. Refrain from blaming others when a problem arises; children already know how to do that. The children will process this information and use it to guide and direct their own behaviors, thoughts, and actions.

Teach children how to be good listeners by being a good listener when they speak to you. Look them in the eye, acknowledge what they say, show interest by nodding and smiling, and ask questions to help them along in their story. Let children be in charge of what they say; do not highjack the conversation, ask too many questions, or repeatedly interrupt.

When speaking with young children, get down on the same level. Rather than standing and staring down at them, sit or kneel down, and talk with them face-to-face. Have the child's attention before speaking with him or her.

Refrain from calling children from across the room. Go over to them and speak. A young child's world is directly in front of him or her, so talk eye-to-eye.

It is often prudent to use young children's names during a conversation to hold their attention. Children tend to "zone out" after a few words. However, when they hear their name, they re-establish their focus and listen. Some children need to hear their name a dozen times over a 2-minute exchange to maintain focus. If that is what it takes, do it.

Use short and simple sentences, and remember to follow the three-word rule using a friendly tone. Nicely remind them to "eat your lunch," keep "hands to yourself," or "get your coat." Always pepper speech with "please," "thank you," and "you're welcome," even if it goes over the word limit. Those words will be heard at a different level of consciousness. Lastly, when speaking with young children, fluctuate the pitch and tone of your voice. They respond best to "sing-song" or melodic tones.

Practicing Solid Teaching

Our job is to capture children's interest, encourage their efforts as they embark on new discoveries, and generate successful learning experiences that build confidence and competence. Create a positive space for children to discover personal independence and self-expression. Acknowledge them as individuals and validate who they are and what they know. Encourage initiative and support their efforts to learn. The joy of learning lies in the process of exploration and discovery. Monitor that learning with gentleness and teach each child to value him- or herself and his or her own work and accomplishments. A positive classroom environment enables a child to have a better sense of self.

Use thoughtful words. When we tell children, "That was good thinking," or "Wow, you really used your brain," they feel smart. If, on the other hand, we say, "What on Earth are you doing? Can't you do anything right?," they feel inadequate. Monitor facial expressions as well. A disapproving look says volumes.

Each day, strive to give children loving care, security, and acceptance. Demonstrate personal responsibility and model appropriate behaviors, so they know how to act. Offer them good options so they can make prosocial choices. Avoid judgment so they learn effective social skills. Teach patience and appreciation so they have high-quality relationships. Show them how to "own" their feelings and work through them so they have a good handle on them as they mature. Be empathetic and respectful so they feel valued by others. Give them a firm foundation on which they can build.

Children will meet our expectations and fulfill the role we define. They can meet high expectations just as easily as low ones, so aim high. Make clear requests, and keep messages positive and productive. Provide encouragement, appreciation, and acknowledgment. They need to be listened to and respected. They need to feel accepted and understood. We can do that!

On difficult days, it helps to think back on our own experiences as children and stand for a moment in their place. Remember how hard some things were to learn and master, then help young children cope by being calm and having patience. Recall those moments of sadness, fear, or feeling completely alone or out of control, then hug them to help them feel secure. Always give them the guidance that they need.

The Power of Touch

Our society has become afraid of touch. We view it with distrust or disdain, and we fear misinterpretation. We shy away from others, keep our distance, and stay in our own 36-inch bubbles. We refrain from touching and apologize when we do. Yet touch is necessary. Touch connects, fosters closeness, and provides a sense of security, especially when we are small. Young children require it on a daily, sometimes hourly, basis to handle stress and cope with change.

Too often, we refrain from hugging a child for fear of lawsuits and are reluctant to touch anyone because it could lead to problems. With all the cases of child abuse, pedophilia, and sexual harassment on the news, one is afraid to even brush against someone. Repulse that negative social pressure, remember the healing quality of touch, and reach out. However, remember that touch should *never* be used to harm, hurt, or in any way jeopardize a child's mental, physical, or emotional health.

When we are comfortable touching people and being touched by others, we can let people know that by reaching out to shake hands, and extending ourselves. Ask permission before touching another person. When meeting a new adult, extend a hand halfway and let the other person complete the connection if they choose to do so. Some people do not welcome touch. Do not take that personally; there might be a reason for their reluctance.

Ask very young children if they want to be held before scooping them up. If they do, they will reach up to show they are willing. If they don't want to be held, respect that.

What about older children? Once again, ask their permission. Remember that they have rights. Respect them. We can not overrule their rights just because we want to relocate them or hug them. If they are willing to be touched, that is one thing. If not, refrain.

One time, a 4-year-old boy bumped his head. It clearly hurt; he quickly put his hand on the spot and started rubbing it. I could have gone over and scooped him up, but instead I asked if he wanted a hug. He vehemently shook his head and said "No!" The motherly "me" wanted to give him one anyway, but the professional "me" stepped back and said, "I can see it really hurts. I will give you a hug when you are ready for one, okay?" He nodded his head.

A few minutes passed, and he composed himself, slowly walked over, and brushed against me. I reached down, squeezed his shoulder, and asked if he wanted his hug now. He nodded and I gave him a squeeze.

Later, it occurred to me why he held off. First, he was in full view of his peers. He already felt foolish about walking into the doorknob. He did not want to be hugged and possibly burst into tears while being comforted, since all of his "4-year-old cool" would be stripped away. Perhaps he feared that some mean-spirited peer would chant "crybaby!" By regaining composure on his own, he managed to put that off.

When children try to connect, be responsive. As a Twos teacher, I learned to walk like a mummy the first few days of school, because my young friends would glom onto my leg and hold on for dear life as I moved about. They thought it was fun to be pulled along as they held tightly to my knees. In fact, it became part of our daily ritual, which helped them adjust to me and the new routine.

My Twos class had a lot of touch time. When I would read a story, there was no "cross-cross applesauce" in my room. I was the "Big V." There I sat on the floor, both legs spread out so three children could sit on each one, two children leaned over my shoulders and one sat in the middle of the V, holding the book and turning the pages. No one was left out; everyone was touching me. As a result, we were spared dozens of arguments over who got to sit on my lap. Everyone had a front-row seat because everyone was seated on me.

In sum, physically extend touch to others. Love the babies, and hug and tickle young children when they are willing. Shake hands with parents and even offer a shoulder to cry on when needed. Pat one another on the back in the classroom and extend a warm and helpful hand when needed. It's easy. Do it.

MEETING THE NEEDS OF ADULTS

In many early childhood education settings, one group of people often goes unnoticed—the *adults* in the community. Who are these adults? They are the staff members and parents, of course. It is always a good idea to make sure that parents, who pay to have their child in a program and have high expectations for their children's success and happiness while there, and the teachers, who provide care and learning opportunities, are treated well and respected.

Parents

Upon enrollment, parents should be given all the information available about the program, its goals, and its policies in writing, verbally, or both. Programs that do not follow this policy often have miscommunications between the parents and staff.

Conduct parent information sessions or open houses in advance of a child's entry, and inform parents and guardians about the program's goals and the expectations for the children. Take questions and make clarifications. Describe in detail the program philosophy and teaching methods. Information at this time determines whether a good match exists between family and school, and will forestall future problems.

Sometimes parents choose a play-based program because they agree with the inherent philosophy, but secretly they want their children to have an academic edge when they go to school. Although this may seem counterintuitive, it happens all the time. Parents know what seems right for the child, but their expectations are not in line. Perhaps they are being pressured by society and media messages. Perhaps they see their child as a mini-adult and expect more from him/her. Perhaps they believe children should learn as much as possible, so time is not wasted. Whatever it is, they just want more than play time.

It is the job of the director and teachers at a program to educate the parents on what is going to take place at their school and in their classroom.

This can be done through handbooks, individual information meetings, orientation evenings, or parent coffee hours.

The Parent Handbook

Clearly state information about the daily curriculum and the expectations for children, as well as the program's mission and goals, and all policies, program practices, and procedures in a parent handbook and distribute it to all families with a signature cover sheet that acknowledges receipt.

The parent handbook should include:

- The preschool philosophy, goals, and objectives and teaching approach (e.g., play-based, academically oriented, Reggio Emilia, Montessori) and sample activities associated with the teaching/ learning method
- An overview of the daily schedule, the weekly classroom routine, and a calendar highlighting holidays and school closures
- Policies outlining physical health standards for the program staff and children, as well policies for refusing entry to sick children, returning to school after illnesses, and time frames for home stay while ill with contagious diseases
- Policies regarding potty-training, diapering, and toileting young children
- Policies for classroom management and/or discipline practices, as well action plans for dealing with behavioral issues, making complaints, and/or removing problematic children, and methods for resolving any issues between the program and the home
- Opportunities for parent involvement
- Staff-to-child ratio and staff qualifications
- Program fees and the process for making timely payment

Parent Involvement

Build a positive parent community by hosting "parent coffee hours" so information can be exchanged. Invite speakers who can discuss child development and early childhood education. Provide workshops to help parents raise their children in positive ways (e.g., effective communication techniques, successful discipline strategies, health and hygiene practices, nutrition counseling).

Arrange field trips and ask family members to chaperone, or invite parents, grandparents, and siblings to come in and do special activities in the classroom (e.g., read a story, play an instrument, do magic tricks, cook a special treat). When family members visit, children get to show their family their school, friends, and teachers, and get to share their family with their peers. On those special days, the child glows with pride and excitement. Family involvement makes a program better.

Lastly, have a format for information exchange. Offer a survey or questionnaire so parents can rate their child's experience across a variety of different dimensions. Ask them to make comments as well as suggestions for improvement.

Go one step further and organize a parent advisory board. This pseudo-PTO can provide good feedback to the program, enhance the relationship between home and school, serve as a vehicle for fundraising, and utilize the skills that parents bring to the program.

Information exchange can be reciprocal. When situations such as sudden unemployment, family issues, or difficulties providing for care/feeding arise, administrators can help families connect to appropriate agencies, make referrals for services, provide information on housing possibilities, or locate a community agency or child advocate. Furthermore, administrators can direct the parents of children with developmental delays or learning problems to appropriate programs within the community, such as Birth to Three, or school district, such as Preschool Services.

The Teaching Staff

Before anything else is offered to the teaching staff—before professional development, before in-service trainings—the one thing every staff member wants is *respect*. Everyone deserves to be treated respectfully. Directors should understand that, parents should provide it, and coworkers should willingly extend it to one another. Volumes could be written on the subject, but suffice it to say that what goes around, comes around. When we treat others with kindness and respect, it will come back to us again and again. When we treat others with disdain and disrespect, we get that squarely back as well.

Parents should respect their child's teachers, and teachers should respect the child's parents. When a mutual, supportive, and respectful relationship is established between home and school, the child truly benefits.

Within the teaching team, strive to create the best early education experience possible. Be supportive of one another. Treat all coworkers with respect and kindness. Share ideas and experiences, and respect those of colleagues, so the children benefit. Be an example to the children, the parents, coworkers, and administrators. Show professionalism at every turn and demonstrate that everyone is worthy of respect.

Resources for Teachers

Provide the basic necessities so the teachers can do a good job. Give them a staff handbook so they know the program's missions, goals, and objectives. Provide clear job descriptions and clearly state the rules for conduct (e.g., no smoking, no personal calls during work, punctual arrival). Outline procedures and practices endorsed by the program, and the policies for removal should a teacher not comply. Include a school calendar, designating holiday time and scheduled school closings, as well as required professional days for staff training. Supply general information on salary or hourly wages and information on benefits, if offered. Delineate any additional employment obligations, such as required health screening and physicals, educational standing, degree requirements, and expectations for professional development and training. These and any other clarifications necessary for employment should be presented in the staff handbook. That way, everyone starts the job on the same page.

Upon hiring a new staff member, conduct a thorough orientation and have the new teacher shadow a more experienced teacher to get a feel for what will be required. Most programs have a probation period for new hires to see if it's a good match. Support the new teacher and give him or her a leg up when needed. It pays off in the end when everyone tries to make the situation work.

Physical Plant

What should the staff have in the physical environment? Start with the basics. Teachers should have a private adults-only bathroom, separate from the one used by the children. No one should have to squat over tiny toilets. Teachers also deserve a secure place to store personal items, such as purses, lunches, coats, aprons, and shoes/slippers. Provide more than a hook on the door or wall; provide a lockable cabinet or closet. It will give teachers peace of mind when they leave their classroom and their valuables.

Place an adult-sized chair in the room, as an alternate to those tiny child-sized chairs, and give teachers' bad backs and aching knees a reprieve. Even if it is just a folding chair in the corner, it's an option for those who need it.

Provide a nice space for teachers to go when taking breaks, such as a lounge that is warm, somewhat private, and comfortable, complete with adult-sized chairs and a table where they can write or eat. Ideally, supply a microwave and refrigerator so they can prepare their food and a teacher resource area with written materials and/or Internet access, so they can access information about child development, early childhood education practices, curriculum, or interpersonal relationships.

What should be available in the classroom? Teachers need ample storage for classroom materials, teacher materials, assessment portfolios, and children's files (e.g., a separate storage closet, storage shelves in the room or in alcove areas) so materials do not have to be precariously stacked all around the room.

Resources: Supportive Experts

Aside from provisions for personal and professional needs, teachers need opportunities for education and access to experts who can answer their questions and help them find solutions to problems. Connect caregivers/ teachers to knowledgeable people from the surrounding community who can provide information, insight, and ideas for dealing with the daily issues that come up in child care and early childhood education.

Health and safety. In advance of the school year, all teachers should have a refresher course in emergency care and practice (e.g., first aid, CPR, administration of medications, use of the epipen). Teachers should be trained to recognize a general allergic reaction, anaphylactic shock (severe allergic reaction), and seizure. A record indicating completion of the training should be kept in each teacher's employment file. Opportunities for teachers to confer with a nurse or registered medical professional (who is onsite to periodically review the health records of the children and staff) should be arranged as needed (suspected pinkeye or chicken pox, etc.). Periodically, these health professionals can also review good hygiene practice (hand-washing techniques, proper health procedures for diapering/toileting, food preparation, and general cleanliness).

Bring in a nutritionist to advise parents and staff about dietary issues, so healthy food choices can be made for snack and cooking activities, and about allergies and food issues, so safe food options are available.

Education support. An education consultant can provide information to staff about early childhood development and education, classroom management practices, curriculum adoption and implementation, and effective communication techniques. Ask the consultant to give staff training and workshops on pertinent issues and review general information about child development and early education so they can keep their goals and objectives in line with the maturational abilities of the children.

Every teacher and caregiver should be apprised of the development and capabilities of both typical and atypical children. Since more children with special needs and circumstances are being included and integrated into a standard preschool setting, teachers need information and support to enable a good fit for the atypical child and the class as a whole.

Thus, it is imperative that teachers understand the special needs that accompany children with developmental, sensory, motor, and/or speech issues. Workshops that are both general and specific to a child's needs should be offered to the staff, program-wide. Do not limit the information to the teachers who are currently working with the child; open it up to those who will get this child in the future (Threes, Fours, and pre-K classrooms), as well as those that might have his or her siblings.

Educate the staff about different cultural backgrounds, ethnicities, and heritages. Be respectful of and well-versed in the different personal, familial, and cultural lifestyles represented by the children in the preschool. Do not assume that all people are alike, or that all people must conform to one approach or standard of living.

Despite years of education or experience, all teachers occasionally have issues with discipline and classroom management, around communication, or problems with parents or coworkers. For those times, hire a knowledgeable professional development trainer who can answer questions and present new approaches or ideas to the staff. Keep good records of all training programs to satisfy state license requirements.

When a director hires knowledgeable professionals to come to the program and offer solid and helpful information, the staff becomes more knowledgeable and, in turn, are better prepared to face issues as they arise and ready to work with all types of children safely and successfully.

Professional Development

Administrators should make conferences and programs outside of the school setting available to the staff by either paying the cost or providing time off to attend. Whenever possible, attend community workshops and statewide or national conferences. Share any information that was gained in these forums with the whole group.

Join organizations related to early childhood education. Enroll in the National Association for the Education of Young Children (NAEYC) and utilize their resources and publications (*Young Children* and *Beyond the Journal*). Purchase books and subscribe to periodicals on a variety of topics and keep them onsite.

> **Point**—Consider hosting an educational program for parents or teachers at the preschool and in the general community.

Finally, encourage teachers to earn more credentials and attain new educational goals. Every day, the world changes a little more. Society has changed so much in the past 50 years that it seems as if parents and grandparents are talking different languages based on their own experiences. Stay current in the field, discover new teaching techniques, explore different types of curricula, and stay open to new ideas.

11

Honorable Mentions
and Memorable Moments

Although I have observed many really wonderful learning experiences and worthwhile interactions from my little chair in the corner, some deserve special acknowledgment and mention.

". . . A BIG BROTHER TO A NEW BABY NAMED MEREDITH"

There once was an absolutely fabulous teacher who personalized her statements rather than using generic comments while transitioning between activities, thereby creating real connections with them. For example, she would say, "Whoever has a new baby sister named Meredith, go to the sink," instead of "Whoever is wearing red, go wash your hands," and the child would raise his hand and shout, "That's me!," racing to the sink.

She incorporated family pet names (e.g., ". . . has a dog named Sparky"), weekend getaway plans (e.g., ". . . is visiting Grandma"), parent occupations (e.g., ". . . whose daddy is a firefighter"), and/or little facts about individual children (". . . has a stuffed lizard named Oliver"), and every time, the child popped alive, savoring the special moment. With each statement, she was saying, "I care about you. You are special to me." This enhanced the teaching relationship, for the children felt that they mattered and became more invested in the learning process and in her as a teacher. It was not the typical "I like my teacher" thing. It went beyond that to a different level of respect and connection. When we create personal and meaningful connections, we win 80% of the battle, because children willingly pay attention, respond to what we say, and listen to our requests.

In kind, when teachers are not human voids, but share parts of their lives, such as that they own a pet iguana or live on a houseboat, children catch a glimpse of the real person, and the relationship becomes more individual. Rest assured that this information is probably a topic of conversation with Mommy in the car or with the whole family over dinner, which is wonderful because the child is enthusiastic about preschool connections and experiences.

THE WALL OF WELCOME

A classroom had a wonderful wall that said "Welcome" in every native language spoken by the families in the classroom (including English, Spanish, Polish, Mandarin Chinese, two Indian dialects, Portuguese, Russian, Jamaican, Creole, and Albanian). Every person who entered the room was welcomed in a personally meaningful way. It doesn't take much to make people to feel good about a place.

THE FAMILY SHRUB

Personalize the classroom space by adding family photos. As the old adage goes, "A picture paints a thousand words." Why not brighten the space with them?

Some programs have sheets of paper filled with family photos; others have families create a "me" collage for each child; yet others display a family tree and put family photos on the various branches. Usually, the pictures are too high for the children to directly see; the display favors the adults.

Instead, make a shrub for each family, using the same concept as the family tree. By having it closer to the ground, the children can sit by their loved ones during times of stress or sadness. Take photos of family members when they visit the room, and integrate them into the display. This underscores the home–school connection, making the child feel at home in both places.

Where can we display family shrubbery? In addition to wall space, utilize the backs of shelf units or storage cabinets, allocate small sections of wall space to each child, or line the inside of each child's cubby space with pictures. However it is done, it will personalize the room. Have a bush for each teacher, too, so everyone is represented.

"LOOK! I'M A GARDEN!"

We all have height charts in our room. Children love to see how much they grow. One center took the height chart to a new level by measuring the children by using 4-inch paper flowers.

First, the children made paper flowers from precut parts that the teacher made and decorated them any way they wished. Once finished, the teacher hung the flowers in a vertical line from the floor up. Above the flower lines there was a caption: "How many flowers tall are you?"

Each child had his or her own "flower line," and the teacher measured each child using the flowers, as the children stood with their backs to the wall. One child turned around after being measured, looked at the long line of flowers, then enthusiastically exclaimed, "Hey! Look! I'm a garden!"

HUMAN ALPHABET PICTURES

Two teachers included children in the creation of a picture alphabet. They believed it would make them more interested in learning their letters. Were they ever right!

The teachers had their work cut out for them when they decided to create a human alphabet using the children. One teacher stood precariously on a ladder while the other happily twisted and turned 18 four-year-olds into 26 different letter shapes. On average, three or four children were used in each letter. Even though they were not used for every letter, the children were all excited, and the enthusiasm was evident in the pictures.

After 26 "clicks" of the camera and a lot of patient effort, the alphabet was ready to hang. After gaggles of giggles, the children helped put the letters in the correct order on the wall. It spanned the length of the room, was the topic of conversation for many days, and was a huge hit with the parents.

WHEN YOU WANT SOMEONE'S ATTENTION, WHISPER!

A child was screaming to get the teacher's attention. The teacher came over, stood right next to her, and whispered that she could use her inside voice because the teacher was right by her. The little girl immediately whispered back to the teacher. The teacher said, "For such a little girl, you have a powerful voice." After that, she would whisper to the teacher.

THE COW FROM CHINA

Ever noticed how many things are marked with the words "Made in China"? One little girl did. She sat happily in the circle area reading a farm story aloud to her teacher by slowly sounding out the words and showing the pictures as she turned the pages. When she finished, the teacher suggested that she get the plastic farm animals and act the story out with them. She heartily agreed.

The teacher left her side but maintained a loose connection by occasionally smiling and looking at her while she played. At one point, the child looked at her with a quizzical expression. The teacher asked, "What's up?"

The little girl looked at the plastic cow figure, then at the teacher, and said, "This cow comes from China!" The teacher asked, "How do you know?"

The child stood up, walked over to the teacher, pointed at the raised lettering on the plastic cow's belly, and declared, "'Cause I can read it!"

BOOK BINS WITH PLAY MATERIALS

A teacher believed that children would be more inclined to actively read if free play were directly connected with books, so she encouraged them to play with materials while looking at picture books. As a result, they would utilize both for long stretches of time. First, they would look at the book and figure out the story through the pictures, if they didn't already know it, then reenact it with the plastic figures. Sometimes the story was repeated verbatim; other times it morphed into a new tale. Over time, a whole new story often emerged. New authors and playwrights emerged, along with their casts of plastic actors. Substitute puppets and flannel board pieces achieve the same end.

SHOE PARKING

Where are the children's shoes placed during naptime? One preschool had a unique way of dealing with shoe storage, as a teacher created a shoe parking lot in the hallway. She had a little space along the wall where each child's name and photo was posted. Little yellow lines were placed on the floor designating the "shoe parking space." As the children returned to the classroom, after their brief pre-nap potty stop, they would take off their shoes and put them in their parking spaces.

One child liked to stay in the hall an extra minute to neaten the shoes. The teacher said that since he did such a great job, he could be the parking attendant. He was thrilled!

WALLACE THE WORM

A skillful teacher used a small finger puppet to assist children in adopting prosocial behaviors. Wallace the Worm was a green finger worm protruding from an apple hand puppet. During morning meeting, the teacher presented the puppet so the children could say "hi" to Wallace. When they reached out to touch him, she reminded them to be gentle so he didn't get hurt and to speak quietly so he didn't get scared.

The children treated Wallace carefully and respectfully, and learned to be kind and compassionate to things that were smaller than themselves.

BUNK BEDS IN DRAMATIC PLAY

In one center, a clever adult constructed a boxed bunk-bed unit for the children to use for rest and dramatic play. There was a bottom bunk, with a thick cushion that filled the entire box space. About 30 inches above the floor was a second-level bunk bed with its own cushion. A small ladder was nearby to access it. Children who liked to climb were encouraged to go there rather than climb on "unauthorized" furniture.

While in the space, children could look at books, rest when they were tired, or just take a break. Since it was self-contained, it was a great space for privacy and quiet.

It also made for some interesting and creative dramatic play. Three children pretended that they were on a long train trip and had to stay overnight in a sleeper car. In today's world of cars and planes, who would travel on a sleeper train? I know three children who would, given the chance.

LITTLE SUITCASES IN DRAMATIC PLAY

The same center that had the bunk beds had a small set of luggage— perfectly sized for young children. They must have been small cosmetic cases (with hard shells) that were either purchased or donated, but either way, they encouraged a great deal of travel and vacation play in the room.

ICE FISHING

Creative teachers should be commended for the wonderful and imaginative planning they do to enhance the play areas for young children.

While teaching a unit on cold weather climates, a group was invited to go "ice fishing" at the sensory table. A few crude fishing poles were made using dowels and string. On one end of the string was a magnet.

The teacher filled the water table with large chunks of ice and added some pieces of Styrofoam to simulate icebergs. While the children tried to "catch" the hidden fish (complete with magnet-attracting paperclips), the teacher talked about cultures where people fish in frozen lakes. She also talked about the sea life that swims under the ice, such as fish, seals, sea lions, and penguins. I was fascinated by the whole lesson. It was a brilliant and original way to present a topic.

THE SHUTTLE TO AFRICA

Four children, seated in a line of four chairs, pretended to be riding a bus. A teacher asked, "What is happening here?" The children said, "We are riding on a bus." "Where are you going?" she asked. One child responded, "Africa."

The teacher smiled and said, "You can't take a bus to Africa. That's across the ocean. You have to take a plane." So the children said, "We are on a plane." They invited her to come along, so she added a chair. She asked who was "driving" the plane. The child seated next to her said she was. The teacher then said, "You can't be. You are sitting with the passengers; you have to be up front." So the group rearranged the chairs into two rows with one in the front.

The teacher then asked what they were holding on their laps. They said, "Our luggage." She said that luggage belongs in the cargo hold, not in the cabin with the people. So, they moved it to the space behind them. She smiled.

A child in a remote part of the room called to the teacher, so she asked if the plane had taken off yet. They said no, so she said she had to get off the plane but she would meet them in Africa later.

While she was at the other end of the classroom, the small group pretended to call the teacher on the phone. She pretended to answer and asked to whom was she speaking. They said they all had called her. She asked how they were all talking at the same time. (Their response was classic: "Speakerphone.") They asked her to come back soon because they were about to blast off. She said, "Planes don't blast off; they take off." One child shouted, "We know that! We are on the shuttle," and then the group started the countdown: "3 . . . 2 . . . 1 . . . Blastoff!" The teacher laughed. Never underestimate the power of dramatic play.

Aside from the fact that the play was rich with imagination and creativity, it was also a great way to introduce new vocabulary as well as to explain and extend experiences. The teacher did an excellent job providing information and giving the group new words to describe the scenario. She also laughed a lot and had fun with the children, which made them want to continue the game all the more. This was a job well done.

THE DANCING GORILLA GOES ON VACATION

Send a classroom prop home with the children so they can write stories about it with their families. It is a great way to encourage children to write and be self-expressive.

One center had a stuffed dancing gorilla. Each week, a child could sign the gorilla out for an adventure. The family had to write a story about the dancing gorilla's time with them. The results were wonderful!

The gorilla had a full album of adventures by the time the school year ended. This gorilla went on family vacations to Disney World, rode on rollercoasters, enjoyed family dinners in the dining room, took long car rides wearing a seat belt, had some interesting encounters with family pets, attended a number of birthday parties (complete with party hats and noisemakers), and spent many a night tucked under the covers alongside an adoring child.

Children enjoyed creating adventures for the gorilla, learned the responsibility of caring for another, and wrote many interesting tales that the class adored. The activity also made the parents a part of the program and allowed them to do "school" things with their child. It was a great addition to the curriculum and truly a job well done.

INSTRUMENTAL MUSIC TO BUILD PUZZLES BY

One teacher believed that soothing music played during quiet-time activities (e.g., table toys, drawing, or writing and puzzle building) could lead to more productive learning experiences. She was right. When she played classical music quietly in the background, more children chose to go closer to the music source and do table activities. Music can be a great tool in creating a positive learning environment.

INTRODUCTION OF PAINTBRUSHES: MOMMY, DADDY, BABY BROTHER

In the art area, a teacher talked with a small group of children as they put on smocks to paint. Rather than directing the art experience, she asked them what type of paintbrush each wanted to use. She showed them three different brushes—a wide sponge brush, a long-fanned bristle brush, and a small stubby-handled brush. They could not decide, so she introduced them to the group. First, she held up the long-fanned brush, and said this is "Papa brush." Next, she held up the sponge brush and called it the "Mama brush." Then, while holding the stubby-handled brush, she identified it as "Baby brush." After that, the children easily decided which brush they would paint with.

FIELD TRIPS

Field trips are integral in the education process. Since children come from a diverse range of experiences, they often do not have the same opportunities outside of the classroom. In order for children to truly understand the big world, they need to see it firsthand. Even if it is just a trip to the post office, they experience it rather than just hearing about it.

One group of children visited a child-friendly "please touch" museum. One area displayed community helpers with different props and dress-up clothes that were accessible to the children. While there, the children tried on the different career costumes and an eager teacher took photos of individuals across careers.

In a different area, children could look through telescopes and microscopes, build complex structures with huge blocks, dance on colored light-up squares, and paint with shadows and light. They had ample opportunities to experience a whole range of things. The teachers took pictures of everything the children did that day.

When the group returned to the classroom, the walls were plastered with photos from the museum trip, with captions beneath many that said "Look what I can do! Look what I can be when I grow up!" This was a great way to open up future possibilities to the children in a personally meaningful way.

BOXES . . . BOXES . . . BOXES!

A teacher kept a bunch of different-sized cardboard boxes and cartons in the room for building. Rather than limiting the children to blocks, she provided materials to make life-sized houses. The children loved this activity. When finished, they would sit inside their box structures.

Initially, each child put together a single box each and sat inside it. When they came together, they built more complex structures using multiple boxes, yielding a larger space where many children could play. Where there were open gaps, they used the flattened boxes to make roofs and doors. They were ingenious in their construction. They stayed there for over an hour, just shaping and reshaping the space.

THREE . . . TWO . . . ONE . . . BLASTOFF!

A rocket balloon—a simple concept and a great deal of fun! The teacher had long balloons that she pumped full of air. The children counted the pumps. When it was filled to capacity and about to fly away, she gave it to a child and asked him to be in charge of sending it off, which basically meant holding the end and then letting it go. The children would then watch it go all around the room. They would shout if it was making a noise or not. Another child retrieved it when it landed. These jobs—sending off the balloon and retrieving it—were used as special acknowledgment for a good day's work.

COOPERATION TAUGHT AND LEARNED

Even though teachers were available to help the children, from the first day on, the teachers encouraged the children to help one another. As a result, the older children in the group, or the ones who had mastered a task, often helped their friends.

A group of 3-year-olds and 4-year-olds were in the same group. When the time came to go outdoors, friends helped each other zip up their coats. When younger children needed help, the teacher asked the older children who knew how to zip to raise their hands so the younger ones could go to them. Shoe-tying was another peer-help partnership. It was a great way to acknowledge a learned skill, give the accomplished learners a chance to "shine," and the younger ones the help they needed from their peers.

THE SONG OF "LIFE"

A child tried to sing a song along with the group. He got all teary-eyed, proclaiming, "I don't know the words." The teacher offered to sing it with him again. He said, "No, I want to do it later." She offered to sing it in the afternoon. He said no. He wanted to do it at home. "I don't know the words," he said again. "Could you give me a list of it?" She smiled. The teacher said she would give him a list and he could go over it with his daddy so he could learn it with him.

This was a sensitive thing for the teacher to do. The little guy wanted to be like everyone else, who knew the words, and he didn't want to showcase his lack of knowledge by learning the song with the teacher. She understood his unease and took the time to teach his dad the words at pickup so they could go over it again and again at home or in the car until the child mastered it.

LET 'EM BE!

During community helper month at school, a teacher placed fire hats and a hose with a conical sprayer on one end in the block area to promote firefighter play. Instead of using it as a hose, a child held the sprayer up to his ear and spoke into the other end. He laughed when he heard himself through the hose. He handed the conical end to another child, who held it up to his ear. The first boy talked into the hose and both fell over laughing when the second boy heard his words. Before long, a group of five children was in the block area talking to one another through the hose. It was not what the teacher had intended, but she watched them and said, "Now that's innovation!"

A . . . B . . . C . . . ON THE COMPUTER

Sometimes, a child's best moments are self-contained, even if onlookers can enjoy it, too. A child wearing headphones sat at the computer working with an alphabet program. When the program prompted her to "sing along with the alphabet song," she did, as loudly as she could. Everyone in the room stopped, looked at her, and smiled as she proudly sang along at top volume. She was totally unaware of the impact she was having.

"HEIGH-HO . . . IT'S OFF TO WORK WE GO"

I once entered a classroom where the children were all busily engaged at a variety of centers, playing in every corner of the room and having a lot of fun. The teacher signaled it was time to stop what they were doing, put away the things they were playing with, and come to circle for morning meeting. The whole group burst into song at once, singing, "Heigh-Ho . . . It's off to work we go" as they cleaned up the various centers.

HOME DEPOT PAINT STRIPS

Once, a group of 4-year-old girls were playing and would not let a fifth girl join the play. The rejected child cried to the teacher, "They said I can't play because my skin is a different color." Everyone in this center was African American—the children and the teachers—so the teacher was surprised by that statement.

She asked the girls why they had said that and the girls, all with darker complexions, said the other girl was not the same color as them, so they did not want to play with her. The small group was split up and sent to different areas to prevent any more discussion like that.

On her way home, the teacher went to the Home Depot paint department. She picked up a number of paint strips to use for a small-group meeting.

Early the next day, she brought the five little girls together to do a special project. She pulled out four paint strips—one with shades of yellow, one with shades of pink, one with shades of blue, and one with shades of brown. She took the yellow one and asked the girls to look at the yellows, varying in color from light to dark, and asked if they liked the color. They all said "yes" and commented on the pretty tones. She asked if they could point out the shade they liked the most. They each pointed to different shades of yellow. She asked if they should play in different groups because they liked different shades of yellow, and they adamantly said no.

She repeated the process with the pink strip. She asked different questions to assess whether one shade was better or worse that any other and if the paint strip should be ripped apart so the colors did not have to be together. Once again, the group was unwilling to separate the colors and said they belonged together even if they were a little different. She did the same general thing with the shades of blue and found the same results.

Then she took out the brown strip. She showed it to the girls and asked if they liked this color strip. They did. She asked if they liked any one color on the strip, and a few chose the lighter shades of brown over the darker ones. She asked if the colors should be taken apart and not kept on the same strip and they said "No!" She asked each child to put a finger next to the brown tone that was closest to their own skin color. They all did. Four children put their fingers near the darker brown. One child put hers near the lighter brown.

The teacher summed up the meeting by saying, "You liked the shades of yellow and thought they all looked pretty together. You liked the pinks and said that no shade was better or worse than any other. You did not think that the blue strip colors should be cut apart. And a few of you pointed to the lighter-color browns on the paper strip when I asked which one you liked the most. If the colors on the paper are good together, so are the colors of our skin. Go play nicely with each other and stop saying that someone does not belong because they are a little different!"

As far as I am concerned, this was not just a memorable moment, but a home run right out of the park. We all could learn from this teacher!

We all can rise to high levels of practice. We all have the ability to make a learning situation meaningful and memorable. Always keep that goal in sight.

We are the luckiest people in the world because we get to see wonder daily in the eyes of young children. They are so willing to believe us, to trust us, to follow us, and to share their enthusiasm for living and their excitement for learning every day. We have to remember that we are in a trusted position. We are partnering with parents to raise our next generation. This is no small role! Assume it to the fullest. Make a firm commitment to be the best influence possible for these impressionable young children.

We prepare children by teaching them how to express themselves, understand their emotions, and gain control over them; by supporting them as they adjust to the larger social context; and by helping them acquire new skills and master them over time. We are active facilitators. Our consistent goal should be to expand the children's experience to encompass big horizons—one activity, book, and conversation at a time.

I once was told by a wise mentor that we should not tell preschool teachers that they are surrogate parents, because the realization of that responsibility might be too overwhelming. I respectfully disagree. Every person who plays a role in a child's life should be completely aware of it and the awesome responsibility that comes with the job. We are not doing a simple job that anyone can do. We are doing an extremely important job, so we should do it right!

I hope something contained within this book has simultaneously touched both your head and your heart and has caused you to stop and think—maybe it brought a memory to mind and made you smile, maybe a section inspired you to try a new approach, maybe you are considering setting up your program in a new way. Whatever it is, I ask you to act upon it. Don't just let the inspiration pass or the desire fade. *Do* something! Ninety percent of making a change is the awareness that something needs to be done differently; the last 10% is doing it.

If something struck a chord in you and is resonating at a different level, move to include this new understanding in your daily life. Good teachers empower others to do good things. Hopefully, something here has made an impression on you and will lead to a more productive and positive experience with young children. If you take away one thing from this book and make the life of children better, then *we* have accomplished *our* goal. Each positive thing we do, each productive change we make, ripples on through others and through time.

It's just one more choice we make; we are completely responsible for each and every one that emanates from our mind and results in a word or action. Just like the children we teach, we have to make good choices and live with the consequences of those choices.

Recommended Reading

Anderson, M. P. (2005). Living with disappointment: How to choose powerful outcomes in the face of unmet expectations. *Exchange, 162,* 49–51.

Baghban, M. (2007). Scribbles, labels and stories: The role of drawing in the development of writing. *Young Children, 62*(1), 20–28.

Berl, P. S. (2005). Mature teachers matter. *Exchange, 165,* 10–14.

Blaska, J. K., & Lynch, E. C. (1998). Is everyone included? Using children's literature to facilitate the understanding of disabilities. *Young Children, 53*(2), 36–38.

Brazelton, T. B., & Sparrow, J. D. (2006). *Touchpoints—Birth to three* (2nd ed.). Cambridge, MA: DeCapo Press.

Brazelton, T. B., & Sparrow, J. D. (2001). *Touchpoints—Three to six.* Cambridge, MA: Perseus.

Bruno, H. E. (2005). At the end of the day. *Exchange, 165,* 66–69.

Buell, M. J., & Sutton, T. M. (2008). Weaving a web with children at the center. *Young Children, 63*(4), 100–105.

Cryer, D., Harms, T., & Riley, C. (2003). *All about the ECERS.* Lewisville, NC: Pact House Publishing.

Curenton, S. M. (2006). Oral storytelling: A cultural art that promotes school readiness. *Young Children, 61*(5), 78–89.

Curtis, D., & Carter, M. (2005). Rethinking early childhood environments to enhance learning. *Young Children, 60*(3), 34–38.

Dahl, K. (1998). Why cooking in the classroom? *Young Children, 53*(1), 17–24.

Dickinson, P., Lothian, S., & Jonz, M. B. (2007). Sharing responsibility for our children: How one community is making its vision for children a reality. *Young Children, 62*(2), 49–55.

Dodge, D. T., Heroman, C., Charles, J., & Maiorca, J. (2004). Beyond outcomes: How ongoing assessment supports children's learning and leads to meaningful curriculum. *Young Children, 59*(1), 20–28.

Dorl, J. (2007). Think aloud—Increase your teaching power. *Young Children, 62*(4), 101–105.

Drew, W. F., Christie, J., Johnson, J. E., Meckley, A. M., & Nell, M. L. (2008). Constructive play—A value-added strategy for meeting early learning standards. *Young Children, 63*(4), 38–44.

Drew, W., & Rankin, B. (2004). Promoting creativity for life using open-ended materials. *Young Children, 59*(4), 38–45.

Duke, N. K. (2007). Let's look in a book. *Young Children, 62*(3), 12–16.

Epstein, A. S. (2003). How planning and reflection develop young children's thinking skills. *Young Children, 58*(3), 28–36.

Friedman, S. (2005). Environments that inspire. *Young Children, 60*(3), 48–58.

Gaffney, J. S., Ostrosky, M. M., & Hemmeter, M. L. (2008). Books as natural support for young children's literacy learning. *Young Children, 63*(4), 87–93.

Harms, T., Clifford, R. M., & Cryer, D. (2005). *Early childhood environment rating scale–Revised edition.* New York: Teachers College Press.

Harris, L. (2005). Staffing at the child care center. *Exchange, 165,* 70–73.

Hartzell, M. (2004). Emotional attachment and healthy development. *Child Care Information Exchange, 157,* 80–84.

Heidemann, S., Chung, C. J., & Menninga, B. (2005). When teachers are learning, children are too: Teaching teachers about assessment. *Young Children, 60*(3), 86–92.

Hemmeter, M. L. (2007). We are all in this together: Supporting children's social emotional development and addressing challenging behavior. *Exchange, 176,* 12–16.

Hemmeter, M. L., Ostosky, M. M., Artman, K. M., & Kinder, K. A. (2008). Moving right along: Planning transitions to prevent challenging behaviors. *Young Children, 63*(3), 18–25.

Holland, M. (2004). "That food makes me sick!" Managing food allergies and intolerances in early childhood settings. *Young Children, 59*(2), 42–46.

Humphreys, J. (2000). Exploring nature with children. *Young Children, 55*(2), 16–20.

Kemple, K. M., Batey, J. J., & Hartle, L. C. (2004). Music play: Creating centers for musical play and exploration. *Young Children, 59*(4), 30–37.

Koster, J. B. (1999). Clay for little fingers. *Young Children, 54*(2), 18–22.

Kremenitzer, J. P., & Miller, R. (2008). Are you a highly qualified emotionally intelligent early childhood educator? *Young Children, 63*(4), 106–112.

Leach, P. (1997). *Your baby and child—From birth to age five—Revised edition.* New York: Knopf.

Love, A., Burns, M. S., & Buell, M. J. (2007). Writing: Empowering literacy. *Young Children, 62*(1), 12–19.

Mayer, K. (2007). Emerging knowledge about emerging writing. *Young Children, 62*(1), 34–40.

McDonald, J. (2007). Selecting counting books. *Young Children, 62*(3), 38–42.

McVicker, C. J. (2007). Young readers respond: The importance of child participation in emerging literacy. *Young Children, 62*(3), 18–22.

Oliver, S. J., & Klugman, E. (2004). Speaking out for play-based learning. *Child Care Information Exchange, 155,* 22–27.

Olson, M. (2007). Strengthening families: Community strategies that work. *Young Children, 62*(2), 26–32.

Ordoñez-Jasis, R., & Ortiz, R. W. (2006). Reading their worlds: Working with diverse families to enhance children's early literacy development. *Young Children, 61*(1), 42–48.

Reivich, K. J., & Gillham, J. E. (2005). Raising children who are hopeful. *Exchange, 162,* 44–48.

Robertson, M. (2005). Using the environment rating scales for quality improvement projects. *Exchange, 165,* 23–26.

Ross, M. E. (2000). Science their way. *Young Children, 55*(2), 6–13.

Rothman, J. (2006). Life lessons: Story acting in kindergarten. *Young Children, 61*(5), 70–76.

Scarlett, G. (2005). Building relationships with young children. *Exchange, 162,* 38–40.

Schulz, D. (2004). Building relationships: Early childhood teacher and the community. *Exchange, 159,* 12–14.

Shidler, L. (2002). Things that should make us go hmmmmm!—Listening to what we say to children. *Young Children, 57*(1), 92–94.

Simons, K. A., & Curtis, P. A. (2007). Connecting with communities: Four successful schools. *Young Children, 62*(2), 12–20.

Smith, M. W., & Dickinson, D. K. (2002). *Early language and literacy classroom observation (ELLCO)—Research edition.* Baltimore, MD: Paul H. Brookes Publishing Company.

Szyba, C. M. (1999). Why do some teachers resist offering appropriate open-ended art activities for young children? *Young Children, 54*(1), 16–20.

Teachout, C., & Bright, A. (2007). Reading the pictures: A missing piece of the literacy puzzle. *Young Children, 62*(4), 106–107.

Wardle, F. (2007). Math in early childhood. *Exchange, 176,* 55–58.

Wasik, B. A. (2006). Building vocabulary one word at a time. *Young Children, 61*(6), 70–78.

Index

About the Author

Cindy Rzasa Bess, Ph.D., is a developmental psychologist, an education consultant, and a lecturer who supports educators and parents on a whole range of child development, parenting, and early and middle childhood education issues. In her career, Cindy has facilitated support groups and has made presentations, conducted workshops, and provided keynote speeches throughout the northeastern United States. She served as a college instructor for 10 years, teaching undergraduate courses on child development, infancy, early/middle childhood, adolescence, and marriage and family relationships. Furthermore, Cindy supplemented her experience by providing care for infants/toddlers; by teaching 2-, 3-, and 4-year-old children in preschool; and by serving as a nursery school director. Lastly, Cindy was trained to be an observer and rater using standardized measures, and subsequently became a Trainer of Trainers in the ECERS-R (*Early Childhood Environment Rating Scale–Revised*) for the State Department of Education in Connecticut. Her first book, *The View from the Little Chair in the Corner*, is a culmination of her experience.

Her training is further supplemented at home, where she and her husband, John, have raised their two young adult daughters.